CIVIL PARTNERSHIPS AND THE MARRIAGE (SAME SEX COUPLES) ACT 2013

REVISED EDITION
STEVE RICHARDS

Emerald Guides

© Straightforward Publishing 2014

ISBN

978-1-84716-426-1

Printed by Grosvenor Group London

Cover design by Straightforward Graphics

Contents

Introduction

Introduction

Since the last edition of this book was produced in 2011, significant changes in the law have taken place, in the main the introduction of the Marriage (Same Sex Couples) Act 2013, which became law in July 2013. This book has now been expanded to include the provisions of this Act. The main provisions of the Marriage (Same Sex Couples) Act 2013 are:

1. To allow same sex couples to marry in a civil ceremony;
2. To allow same sex couples to marry in a religious ceremony where the religious organisation has "opted in"
3. To enable civil partners to convert their civil partnership into a marriage;
4. To enable married individuals to change their legal gender without having to end their marriage.

Those couples not in an existing legal relationship will be able to give notice of marriage from **Thursday 13th March 2014**. The first marriage for same sex couples will therefore be able to take place on Saturday 29th March 2014. This does not apply to a couple who are currently in a civil partnership. The arrangements for allowing the conversion of civil partnerships into marriages, and allowing people who change their legal gender to remain in their marriage, will follow later.

Since the introduction of the Civil Partnerships Act 2004, many same sex couples have entered into civil partnerships. The new Act allows those who wish to get married, particularly in a religious setting, to do so. This book covers both the Civil Partnerships Act 2004 and the Marriage (same Sex Couples Act 2013. Chapter one provides an overview of the Civil partnerships Act 2004, whilst chapters 2-9 provide more detailed provisions in the Act. Chapter 10 provides a detailed overview of the 2013 Act. It should act as an ideal introduction to the law and procedure of same sex partnerships and marriage.

Chapter 1.

Overview of the Civil Partnerships Act 2004

This brief introduction provides an overview of the Civil Partnerships Act 2004. It is intended to provide a back ground to the more detailed information provided within the body of the text contained in this book. The information has been updated to 2013.

The book does not cover Scotland or Northern Ireland, which are contained in Parts 3 and 4 to the Act, although there are references to both countries throughout. The Act is similar throughout the United Kingdom, but there are differences to take into account different legal systems. For further details on the Act as it applies in Scotland and Northern Ireland you should go to the government website which displays the Act in its entirety: www. legislation.gov.uk.

Since 2005, the number of civil partnerships has, naturally declined, and the differences in men and women entering civil partnerships has equalised. With the introduction of the Marriage (Same Sex Couples) Act 2013 as described in Chapter 10, it is likely that more couples will, in the first instance, opt to get marriage, although this remains to be seen.

Civil Partnerships

Part 1 of the Civil Partnerships Act 2004 introduces and defines a civil partnership. A Civil partnership is a legal relationship, which can be registered by two people of the same sex. Same sex couples within a civil partnership can obtain legal recognition for their relationship and can obtain the same benefits generally as married couples.

The Civil Partnerships Act came into force on 5th December 2005. The first civil partnerships registered in England and Wales took place on 21st December 2005. Civil partners will be treated the same as married couples in many areas, including:

- Tax, including inheritance tax
- Employment benefits
- Most state and occupational pension benefits
- Income related benefits, tax credits and child support
- Maintenance for partner and children
- Ability to apply for parental responsibility for a child
- Inheritance of a tenancy agreement
- Recognition under intestacy rules
- Access to fatal accidents compensation
- Protection from domestic violence
- Recognition for immigration and nationality purposes

The registration of a civil partnership

Part 2, Chapter 1, of the Act introduces the registration process. Two people may register a civil partnership provided they are of the same sex, not already in a civil partnership or legally married, not closely related and both over 16 although consent of a parent or guardian must be obtained if either of them are under 18. This section of the Act has now been amended by Paragraph 34 of the Marriage (Same Sex Persons) Act 2013 which now states that a widow or widower under 18 does not require consent of another person before entering into a civil partnership.

Registering a civil partnership is a secular procedure and is carried out by the registration service, which is responsible for the registration of births, deaths and marriages. A civil partnership registration is carried out under what is termed a standard procedure, which can be varied to take into account housebound people or people who are ill and are not expected to recover.

The standard procedure for registering a civil partnership

A couple wishing to register a civil partnership just have to decide the date they want to register and where they want the registration to take place. The formal process for registering consists of two main stages-the giving of a notice of intention to register and then the registration of the civil partnership itself.

The first stage, the giving of notice is a legal requirement and both partners have to do this at a register office in the area of a local authority where they live, even if they intend to register elsewhere. The notice contains the names, age, marital or civil partnership status, address, occupation, nationality and intended venue for the civil partnership. It is a criminal offence to give false information. If one of the partners is a non-EAA citizen and subject to immigration controls (see later) there are additional requirements to be fulfilled. Once the notice has been given it is displayed at the relevant register office for 15 days. This provides an opportunity for objections to be made. The civil partnership cannot be registered until after 15 clear days have elapsed from the date of the second person gives notice.

Each partner needs to give notice in the area that they have lived for at least seven days. If the couple live in different areas then each will post a notice in their own relevant area. When giving notice they will be asked where they wish the civil partnership to take place.

Residency requirements for a civil partnerships

A couple can register a civil partnership in England and Wales as long as they have both lived in a registration district in England and Wales for at least seven days immediately before giving notice. If one person lives in Scotland and the other lives in England or Wales, the person living in Scotland may give notice there. Officers, sailors or marines on board a Royal Navy ship at sea can give notice to the captain or other commanding officer, providing they are going to register with someone who is resident in England and Wales. Service personnel based outside England and Wales have to fulfil the above residence requirements.

Documentary evidence of name, age and nationality will need to be shown. Passports and birth certificates are the main documents required. Proof of address will be required. If either partner has been married or in a civil partnership before, then evidence of divorce or dissolution will be required. If either partner is subject to immigration control a document showing entry clearance granted to form a civil partnership will need to be shown, along with a home office certificate of approval and indefinite leave to remain in the UK.

Civil partnership registration

A civil partnership registration can take place in any register office in England and Wales or at any venue that has been approved to hold a civil partnership. Approved premises include stately homes and other prestigious buildings including hotels and restaurants. From 5th December 2005, any venue that has approval for civil marriage will automatically be approved for civil partnerships. A civil partnership cannot be registered on a religious premises. A civil partnership can only be registered between the hours of 8am to 6pm unless one person is seriously ill and is not expected to recover.

A civil partnership is legally registered once the couple have signed the legal document, known as a civil partnership schedule, in the presence of a registrar and two witnesses. On the day, two witnesses will be required. If they wish to do so, the couple will be able to speak to each other the words contained in the schedule:

' I declare that I know of no legal reason why we may not register as each other's civil partner. I understand that on signing this document we will be forming a civil partnership with each other'

A ceremony can be arranged to accompany the actual registration. This ceremony can take place at any venue as long as it is approved. It is prohibited for civil partnerships to include religious readings, music or symbols.

It was originally prohibited for the ceremonies to take place in religious venues. On 17 February 2011, Her Majesty's Government announced that, as the result of the passing of the Equality Act 2010, it would bring forward the necessary measures to remove the latter restriction in England and Wales, although religious venues would not be compelled to offer civil partnerships. This was implemented by The Marriages and Civil Partnerships (Approved Premises) (Amendment) Regulations 2011

Costs of registering a civil partnership

The costs here are applicable to 2013/14. Like all other costs they will change from year to year and the current costs should always be ascertained by contacting your local register office.

The current average costs are as follows:

- Giving notice of intention to register   £30 (£60 per couple)
- Registration at Register Office   £40

Registration at an approved premises-in this case the cost for attendance by a civil partnership registrar is set by the registration authority in question. A further charge may also be made by the owner for use of the building,

- Cost of civil partnership certificate on the day of registration (Average) £3.50
- Further copies of the civil partnership certificate (Average) £7

The General Register Office website www.gro.gov.uk has a search facility if you need to find a local register office or an office any where in the UK.

Changing names

After registering a civil partnership, one partner might want to change their surname to that of their partner. Government departments and agencies will accept civil partnership certificates as evidence for changing surnames. Other private institutions may want a different form of evidence. It is up to the individual to check with the various organisations if they wish to change their surname.

Special circumstances

Variations to the standard procedure can be made in certain circumstances. If a partner is seriously ill and is not expected to recover then a civil partnership can be registered at any time. The 15-day waiting period will not apply. A certificate will need to be provided from a doctor stating that a person is not expected to recover and cannot be moved to a place where civil partnerships take place and that they understand the nature and purpose of signing the Registrar Generals licence.

Housebound people

If one partner is housebound there are special procedures to allow them to register a civil partnership at home. A statement has to be signed, made by a doctor, confirming that this is the case and that the condition is likely to continue for the next three months. The statement must have been made no more than 14 days before notice being given and must be made on a standard form provided by the register office. The normal 15-day period will apply between giving notice and the civil partnership registration.

Detained people

There are special procedures to allow a couple to register a civil partnership at a place where one of them is detained in a hospital or prison. The couple has to provide a statement, made by the prison governor or responsible person confirming that the place where a person is detained can be named in the notice of proposed civil partnership as the place where the registration is to take place. This statement must have been made no more than 21 days prior to notice being given. The normal 15 day waiting period applies.

Gender change

The Gender Recognition Act 2004 enables transsexual people to change their legal gender by obtaining a full Gender Recognition Certificate. Where a transsexual person is married, they cannot obtain a full Gender Recognition Certificate without first ending their existing marriage. However, if they and their former spouse then wish to form a civil partnership with one another without delay, they can do so as soon as the full Gender Recognition Certificate has been issued. In those circumstances, they give notice and register on the same day. More information is available about the process of changing gender on www.grp.gro.uk

Immigration requirements for people subject to immigration controls

The civil partnerships provisions for people subject to immigration control are exactly the same as those in place for marriage. These apply if one partner is a non-EAA (European Immigration Area) citizen and is subject to immigration control, for example in the UK on a visa.

People subject to immigration control who want to give notice of a civil partnership need to do so at a register office designated for this purpose. They are required to produce one of the following as part of that notice:

- entry clearance granted to form a civil partnership
- A Home Office certificate of approval
- Indefinite leave to remain in the UK.

Registrars are required to report any civil partnerships to the immigration service if they have any suspicions.

Application for leave to remain

Civil partners of British citizens and people settled here can apply for an initial period of two years leave to remain in the UK. If they are still together at the end of that period they can apply for indefinite leave to remain.

Work permit holders and students

Civil partners of people with temporary leave to remain in the UK, such as students and work permit holders, can apply for leave along with their civil partners.

A list of Register Offices for people subject to immigration control, can be found at www.ind.homeoffice.gov.uk

Civil partnership registration for two non-EAA citizens

Two non-EAA citizens can register a civil partnership together in the UK as long as they have entry clearance for the purpose of doing so and have resided in the registration district for at least seven days before giving notice. Registering a civil partnership doesn't affect their immigration status.

Registering civil partnerships abroad

If couples wish to register a civil partnership abroad they should contact the Embassy or High Commission in the country concerned. Couples may be asked to obtain a certificate of no impediment.

It may be possible for couples to register at a UK consulate in another country if one of them is a UK national. However, UK consulates will not register civil partnerships if the host country objects or if civil unions or same sex marriage is available in that country.

Armed Forces

Members of the Armed Forces can register civil partnerships overseas in those areas where a Servicing Registering Officer is able to offer this service.

Overseas relationships

It may be the case that a couple has formed a civil union, registered partnership, domestic partnership or same-sex marriage abroad. Couples in those kind of relationships can automatically be recognised in the UK as civil partners without having to register again provided conditions set out in sections 212 to 218 of the Civil Partnership Act are met.

The legislation defines an overseas relationship that can be treated as a civil partnership in the UK as one that is either specified in Schedule 20 to the Civil Partnership Act or one which meets general conditions in the Act and certain other conditions. Schedule 20 of the Act lists countries and relationships that are recognised. Countries listed in the Act are:

- Andorra
- Australia: Tasmania
- Belgium
- Canada-Nova Scotia and Quebec
- Denmark (including Greenland)
- Finland
- France
- Germany
- Iceland
- Luxembourg
- Netherlands
- New Zealand
- Norway
- Sweden
- USA-Vermont-Connecticut-Maine-Massachusetts-New Jersey-California.

The above are correct as at 2014 but should be checked as they are subject to change.

A couple who have formed a relationship recognised in one of those countries can be recognised in the UK as civil partners if they are of the same sex, the relationship has been registered with a responsible body in that country, the couple were eligible to enter into a civil relationship in that country and all procedural requirements have been fulfilled.

For foreign relationships in countries not listed in Schedule 20 a couple who have formed a relationship can still be recognised as civil partners if the foreign relationship meets the general conditions set out in the Civil Partnerships Act.

Dissolution of relationships formed abroad

Where a couple have formed an overseas relationship and that relationship is treated as a civil partnership in the UK, they may be able to obtain a dissolution, annulment or legal separation here. Legal advice should be sought in this matter.

Family relationships

The law now recognises the role of both civil partners in respect of a child living in their household.

Adoption

Under the Adoption and Children Act 2002, which came into force on 30th December 2005, civil partners may apply jointly to adopt a child.

Parental responsibility

Under the Adoption and Children Act 2002, a person will also be able to acquire parental responsibility for the child of their civil partner. They can do this with the agreement of their civil partner. If the child's other parent also has parental responsibility, both parents must agree. Parental responsibility can also be acquired on application to the court. Civil partners will have a duty to provide maintenance for each other and any children of the civil partnership.

Social security, tax credits and child support

Entering into a civil partnership will affect entitlements to the benefits and tax credits a person may be receiving. From 5th December 2005, the income of a civil partner has been taken into account when calculating entitlement to income related benefits. These benefits include income support, income based job seekers allowance, pension credit, housing benefit and council tax benefit. For a list of benefits and other advice contact the Benefit Enquiry Line on 0800 882200.

Tax credits

From 5th December the income of a civil partner has been taken into account when calculating entitlement to child and working tax credits. The Tax Credit Line on 0345 300 3900 can offer further advice.

Child support

From 5th December 2005, civil partners who are parents will be treated in the same way as married partners for child support. Also, parents who are living with a same sex partner even where they have not formed a civil partnership will be treated in the same way as parents who live together with an opposite sex partner but who are not married.

For further information contact the Child Support Agency Helpline on 08456 588683.

Pensions

Survivor benefits in occupational and personal pension schemes. Surviving civil partners will be entitled to a pension based on accrued pension right. New rules for civil partners mean that a surviving partner will benefit from a survivors pension based on the contracted out pension rights accrued by their deceased partner from 1988 to the date of retirement or death if this occurs before retirement. This new rule applies to all contracted out private pension schemes.

State pensions

From 5th December 2005, civil partners have enjoyed most of the same state pension rights as husbands and they will treated the same as husbands and wives after 2010 when the treatment of men and women will be equalised. For more information concerning pensions contact the Pensions Advisory Service on 0845 6012923.

Tax

From 5th December 2005, civil partners have been treated the same as married couples for tax purposes. Information is available from a local tax office and the HMRC website www.hmrc.gov.uk

Employment rights

Employers are required to treat both married partners and civil partners in the same way. The Employment Equality (Sexual Orientation) Regulations 2003 have been amended to ensure that civil partners receive the same treatment and can bring a claim for sexual orientation discrimination if this is not the case. Other areas where changes are made include flexible working, where a civil partner of a child under six or disabled child under 18 will be able to take advantage of flexible working arrangements. Paternity and adoption leave will now be the right of civil partners More information on paternity and adoption leave and pay can be found on www.moneyadviceservice.org.uk.

Wills

Like all people, couples or not, making a will is the most sensible way of ensuring equitable disposal of your assets in accordance with your wishes. The most valuable asset is usually a home and this will automatically vest in a civil partner after death of the other partner, whether or not a will expressly states this. All other property belonging to one of the civil partners will be disposed of according to the will.

If a person has a will and then registers a civil partnership it will be revoked automatically unless it expressly states otherwise.

If a person dies without making a will there are special legal rules which determine how the estate of the deceased should be shared amongst that persons relatives.

Where a person is married or in a civil partnership and has no other surviving close relatives

Where a person dies intestate and leaves a spouse or civil partner who survives the deceased by at least 28 days and the deceased has no surviving children, parents, brothers or sisters or nieces or nephews (half brothers, sisters, nieces and nephews are not included) then the whole of the deceased's estate goes to the surviving spouse or civil partner.

Where a person is married or in a civil partnership and has no children but leaves other surviving close relatives

If the deceased has no children at the time of his or her death but leaves a parent or a brother or sister or a niece or nephew (again half brothers, sisters, nieces and nephews are not included) then the spouse or civil partner will inherit the personal possessions of the deceased plus the first £450,000 of the deceased's estate.

The spouse or civil partner will also receive half of the balance of the deceased's assets over £450,000. The remaining half passes to the deceased's parents, or if he or she has no surviving parents, to his or her brothers and sisters. If the deceased has no surviving parents to brothers and sisters the remaining half passes to any surviving nieces and nephews.

Where a person is married or in a civil partnership and leaves children

If the deceased leaves a child or children the surviving spouse or civil partner will inherit the deceased's personal possessions plus the first £250,000 of the deceased's estate.

The spouse or civil partner has a right to receive an income from half of the balance of the deceased's estate over £250,000.

The remaining half of the balance passes to the deceased's children when they reach the age of 18 or to the deceased's grandchildren if his or her own children die before him or her.

When the spouse or civil partner of the deceased dies the first half of the balance also passes to the children.

Separated and divorced spouses

Where the deceased and his or her spouse or civil partner have been judicially separated the former spouse or civil partner does not inherit anything. Similarly, where a couple have been divorced or a civil partnership has been dissolved the surviving spouse or civil partner does not inherit anything.

Where a person is not married or in a civil partnership and leaves children

Where a person dies intestate and does not leave a spouse or civil partner (or where the spouse or civil dies within 28 days of the deceased) and the deceased has children then the whole of the deceased's estate goes to his or her surviving children.

Where a person is not married or in a civil partnership and has no children

Where a person dies intestate and does not leave a spouse or civil partner (or where the spouse or civil dies within 28 days of the deceased) and the deceased does not have any children then the whole of the deceased's estate goes to his or her surviving parents (step-parents and in-laws are excluded) in equal shares.

If the deceased has no surviving partner, children or parents then the whole of his or her estate will be inherited by the deceased's brothers and sisters (half-brothers and sisters are excluded). If there are no brothers or sisters the deceased's estate passes to any half-brothers and sisters. If there are no half-brothers and sisters the estate passes to the deceased's grandparents. If there are no surviving grandparents it passes to the deceased's uncles and aunts and if there are no surviving uncles and aunts it passes to any half-uncles and aunts.

Where a person dies leaving no surviving close relatives

Where a person dies leaving no surviving spouse or civil partner, no children, siblings or grandchildren and no aunts or uncles the deceased's estate passes to the Crown or the Duchy of Lancaster or the Duke of Cornwall.

The role of the courts

The Courts have the power to override the rules of intestacy where the distribution of a person's estate in accordance with the rules would not adequately provide for family members in certain circumstances.

Life assurance

Civil partners can hold life insurance on their partner's life on the same basis as a married person. In the event of an accident caused by negligence of another then the civil partner can claim compensation and can claim bereavement damages, currently £10,000. Similarly, someone living with the deceased as though they had been in a civil partnership for two years prior to date of death will also be entitled to claim compensation as a dependant.

Tenancy rights

The general effect of the Civil Partnerships Act has been to give the same rights to civil partners as married couples. The Act also equalises the rights of same sex couples who are living together as if they were civil partners and their families with those of unmarried opposite sex couples.

Private sector tenants

The same sex partner of an assured tenant or assured shorthold tenant will have the same rights of succession to a tenancy as those tenants of local authority or registered social landlords. For further information on housing and tenancies visit www.gov.uk

Dissolution of a civil partnership

Part 2, Chapter 2 contains the provisions for the dissolution of a civil partnership. A civil partnership ends only on the death of one of the civil partners, or on the dissolution of the partnership or a nullity odder or a presumption of death order by the court. The Marriage (Same Sex Couples) Act 2013 amends the Civil Partnerships Act and now provides that, in addition to death, dissolution and annulment, a civil partnership ends if it is converted into a marriage under section 9 of the Act.

The usual route is for one of the partners to seek a dissolution order to terminate the civil partnership. Other options are available. If one party, for example, did not validly consent as a result of duress, mistake or unsoundness of mind, then a nullity order may be sought from the court, or if both civil partners do not wish to terminate the partnership one of them may ask the court for a separation order.

The dissolution process

Whoever decides to end the civil partnership should seek legal advice. The case will usually be dealt with by a civil partnership proceedings county court, although complex cases will be referred to the high court.

To end a civil partnership the applicant (petitioner) must prove to the court that the civil partnership has irretrievably broken down. Proof of an irretrievable breakdown is based on the following:

- Unreasonable behaviour by both or other civil partner
- Separation for two years with the consent of the other civil partner
- Separation for five years without the consent of the other civil partner
- If the other civil partner has deserted the applicant for a period of two years or more.

Nullity

In exceptional circumstances one party to a civil partnership may decide to seek a court order (a 'Nullity' order) to annul the civil partnership.

Separation

The grounds on which a separation order may be sought are exactly the same as those for a dissolution order. The end result is different, as a person whose civil partnership has been dissolved is free to marry or form a new partnership whereas a person who has separated remains a civil partner.

Property and financial arrangements

Part 2 Chapter 3 deals with property and financial relationships. If a civil partnership is ending or if the couple are separating, they will need to decide what happens to any property belonging to them. If they agree on a division they can ask the court to approve the agreement. If they cannot agree they can ask the court to decide. The court has power to make a range of orders in relation to property and other assets including income:

- The court can make an order that one civil partner pay maintenance to the other either for the benefit of the civil partner or for the benefit of any children of the relationship. These orders are known as financial provision orders.

- The court can make an order which will adjust the property rights of the civil partners as regards to property and other assets which they own, either together or separately. This may, for example, mean ordering the transfer and ownership of property from one civil partner to another for that persons benefit or the benefit of any children (known as property adjustment orders)

- The court can make an order in relation to the future pension entitlement of one of the civil partners in favour of the other. This order can relate to occupational pensions, personal pensions and other annuities (known as pension sharing orders)

Financial provision orders for maintenance can be made before a civil partnership has been ended or as a separation order granted by the court. Property adjustment and pension sharing orders only take legal effect once dissolution, separation or nullity order has been made by the court.

Even if the couple have been able to agree on maintenance and other property issues they should seek professional advice on such issues. In most cases the solicitor dealing with the end of the civil partnership will be able to provide appropriate advice.

Care of children

Part 2 Chapter 5 deals with the care of children. Agreeing arrangements for the care of any children should be the first priority of couples who are ending their civil partnerships or choosing to live apart through separation.

If a couple decide to end the civil partnership the court will want to ensure that both partners are happy with the arrangements for looking after children. If a couple are unable to agree the court will decide for them, or may do so, as part of the dissolution proceedings.

****

Chapter 2.

Part 1 of the 2004 Civil Partnerships Act

Part 1 Civil Partnership

Subsection (1) Part 1 states that a civil partnership is a relationship between two people of the same sex ("civil partners")-

- a) which is formed when they register as civil partners of each other-

  - (i)   in England or Wales (under Part 2),
  - (ii)   in Scotland (under Part 3),
  - (iii)   in Northern Ireland (under Part 4), or
  - (iv)   outside the United Kingdom under an Order in Council made under chapter 1 of Part 5 (registration at British Consulates etc, or by armed forces personnel), or

- b) which they are treated under Chapter 2 of Part 5 as having formed (at the time determined under that Chapter) by virtue of having registered an overseas relationship.

Subsection (2) states that subsection (1) is subject to the provisions of this Act under or by virtue of which a civil partnership is void.

Subsection (3) states that a civil partnership ends only on death, dissolution or annulment.

Subsection (4) states that the references in subsection (3) to dissolution and annulment are to dissolution and annulment having effect under or recognised in accordance with this Act.

Subsection (5) states that references in this Act to an overseas relationship are to be read in accordance with Chapter 2 of Part 5.

****

Chapter 3.

Part 2. Registration of Civil Partnerships

Formation of civil partnerships by registration

Section 2 Part 2 of the Act deals with formation of civil partnerships by registration. Subsection (1) states that for the purposes of section 1, two people are to be regarded as having registered as civil partners of each other once each of them has signed the civil partnership document-

    a)   at the invitation of, and in the presence of, a civil partnership registrar, and

    b)   in the presence of each other and two witnesses.

Subsection (2) states that subsection 91) applies regardless of whether subsections (3) and (4) are complied with.

Subsection (3) states that after the civil partnership document has been signed under subsection (1), it must also be signed, in the presence of the civil partners and each other, by-

    a)   each of the two witnesses, and

    b)   the civil partnership registrar.

Subsection (4) states that after the witnesses and the civil partnership registrar have signed the civil partnership document, the relevant registration authority must ensure that-

    a)   the fact that the two people have registered as civil partners of each other, and

    b)   any other information prescribed by regulations,

is recorded in the register as soon as is practicable.

Subsection (5) states that no religious service is to be used while the civil partnership registrar is officiating at the signing of a civil partnership document.

Subsection (6) states that "the civil partnership document" has the meaning given by section 7(1).

Subsection (7) states that "the relevant registration authority" means the registration authority in whose area the registration takes place.

Eligibility

Section 3 deals with eligibility of partners to form a civil partnership. Subsection (1) states that two people are not eligible to register as civil partners of each other if

a) they are not of the same sex,
b) either of them is already a civil partner or lawfully married,
c) either of them is under 16, or
d) they are within prohibited degrees of relationship.

The definition of prohibited degrees of relationship is found in Schedule 1 to the Act and means essentially, closely related. There are absolute prohibitions and qualified prohibitions. See appendix for a list of Schedules to Act as outlined in this book. The schedules can be accessed through the government website mentioned in the overview to the Act.

Parental consent where proposed civil partner under 16

Section 4 deals with parental consent where the proposed civil partner is under 18. Although two people aged 16 or over can register for a civil partnership, subsection (1) of section 4 states that consent of an 'appropriate person' is required before a child under 16 and another person may register as civil partners The definition of appropriate person. is to be found in Schedule 2 of the Act. *Paragraph 35 of The Marriage (Same Sex Couples) Act 2013 amends section 4 in that a widow or widower under the age of 18 will not require the consent of another person before entering into a civil partnership.*

The general registration procedure

Section 5 deals with the general registration procedure. There are a number of procedures under which two people may register as civil partners of each other: the standard procedure; the procedure for house bound persons; the procedure for detained persons and the special procedure which is designed for cases where people are seriously ill and not expected to recover.

Standard procedure

The standard procedure is used in most cases and where the other procedures do not apply.

Special procedure

Special procedures will apply where people are seriously ill, as described above. This will involve a variation to the standard procedure to encompass the circumstances of the illness.

The procedure for housebound persons

If one person is housebound there are special procedures to allow them to register a civil partnership at home. A statement has to be signed, by a doctor, confirming that this is the case and that the condition is likely to continue for the next three months. The statement must have been made no more than 14 days before notice being given and must be made on a standard form provided by the register office. The normal 15-day period (see below) will apply between giving notice and the civil partnership registration.

Detained persons

There are special procedures to allow a couple to register a civil partnership at a place where one of them is detained, for example a hospital or prison. The couple have to provide a statement, made by the prison governor or responsible person confirming that the place where a person is detained can be named in the notice of proposed civil partnership as the place where the registration is to take place. The statement must have been made no more than 21 days prior to notice being given. The normal 15 day waiting period applies (see below).

Place of registration

Section 6 of the Act outlines the place of registration for a civil partnership. Subsection (1) states that the place at which two people may register as civil partners of each other-

a) must be in England or Wales,
b) must not be in a religious premises, and
c) must be specified in the notices, or notice, of proposed civil partnership required by this chapter.

Subsection (2) states that "religious premises" means premises which-

a) are used solely or mainly for religious purposes, or
b) have been so used and have not been subsequently used solely or mainly for another purpose.

(On 17 February 2011, Her Majesty's Government announced that, as the result of the passing of the Equality Act 2010, it would bring forward the necessary measures to remove the above restriction in England and Wales, although religious venues would not be compelled to offer civil partnerships. This was implemented by The Marriages and Civil Partnerships (Approved Premises) (Amendment) Regulations 2011).

Subsection (3) states that in the case of registration under the standard procedure (including that procedure modified as mentioned in section 5), the place-

a) must be one which is open to any person wishing to attend the registration, and

b) before being specified in a notice of proposed civil partnership, must be agreed with the registration authority in the area where the place is located.

Subsection (4) states that if the place specified in a notice is not so agreed, the notice is void.

Subsection (5) states that a registration authority may provide a place in its area for the registration of civil partnerships.

The Civil partnership document

Section 7 deals with the civil partnership document. Subsection (1) of section 7 states that in this part "the civil partnership document" means-

a) in relation to the special procedure, a Registrar General's licence, and
b) in relation to any other procedure, a civil partnership schedule.

Subsection (2) states that before two people are entitled to register as civil partners of each other-

a) the civil partnership document must be delivered to the civil partnership registrar, and
b) the civil partnership registrar may then ask them for any information required (under section 2(4)) to be recorded in the register.

The standard procedure
Notice of proposed civil partnership and declaration

Section 8 of the Act deals with the notice of proposed civil partnership and declaration. Subsection (1) states that for two people to register as civil partners of each other under the standard procedure, each of them must:

a) give a notice of proposed civil partnership to a registration authority and
b) have resided in England or Wales for at least 7 days immediately before giving the notice.

Subsection (2) states that a notice of civil partnerships must contain prescribed information. This can be obtained from the appropriate register office.

Subsection (3) states that the notice must also include the necessary declaration, made and signed by the person giving the notice-

a) at the time when the notice is given, and
b) in the presence of an authorised person;

and the authorised person must attest the declaration by adding his/her name, description and place of residence.

Subsection (4) states that the necessary declaration is a solemn declaration in writing-

a) that the proposed civil partner believes that there is no impediment of kindred or affinity or other lawful hindrance to the formation of the civil partnership;
b) that each of the proposed civil partners has had a usual place of residence in England and Wales for at least 7 days before giving the notice.

Subsection (5) states that where a notice of civil partnership is given to a registration authority in accordance with this section, the registration authority must ensure that the following information is recorded in the register as soon as possible-

a) the fact that the notice has been given and the information in it;
b) the fact that the authorised person has attested the declaration.

Subsection (6) states that "authorised person" means an employee or officer or other person provided by a registration authority who is authorised by that authority to attest notices of proposed civil partnership.

Subsection (7) states that for the purposes of this Chapter, a notice of proposed civil partnership is recorded when subsection (5) is complied with.

Power to require evidence of name etc.

Section 9 deals with powers to require evidence of identity. Subsection (1) of section 9 states that the registration authority to which a notice of proposed civil partnership is given may require the person giving the notice to provide it with specified evidence-

a) relating to that person, or
b) if the registration authority considers that the circumstances are exceptional, relating not only to that person but also to the persons proposed civil partner.

Subsection 92) states that such a requirement may be imposed at any time before the registration authority issues the civil partnership schedule under section 14.

Subsection (3) states that "specified evidence" in relation to a person, means such evidence as may be specified in guidance issued by the Registrar General-

a) of the persons name and surname
b) of the persons age,
c) as to whether the person has previously formed a civil partnership or marriage and, if so, as to the ending of the civil partnership or marriage,
d) of the persons nationality, and

e) as to the persons residence in England or Wales during the period of 7 days preceding the giving of a notice of proposed civil partnership by that person.

Proposed civil partnership to be publicised

Section 10 of the Act deals with the publication of the proposed partnership. Subsection (1) of section 10 states that where a notice of proposed civil partnership has been given to a registration authority, the relevant information must be publicised during the waiting period-

a) That registration authority
b) any registration authority in whose area the person giving the notice has resided during the period of 7 days preceding the giving of the notice,
c) by any registration authority in whose area the proposed civil partner of the person giving the notice has resided during the period of 7 days preceding the giving of that notice
d) by the registration authority in whose area the place specified in the notice as the place of proposed registration is located and
e) by the Registrar General.

Subsection (2) states that "the relevant information" means-

a) the name of the person giving the notice,
b) the name of the person's proposed civil partner and
c) any other information prescribed by regulations.

Meaning of "the waiting period"

Section 11 deals with the meaning of the term waiting period. This mean the period-

a) beginning the day after the notice is recorded, and

b) subject to section 12, ending at the end of the period of 15 days beginning with that day.

Power to shorten the Waiting period

Section 12 deals with powers to shorten the waiting period. Subsection (1) of section 12 states that if the Registrar General, on an application being made to him, is satisfied that there are compelling reasons because of the exceptional circumstances of the case for shortening the period of 15 days mentioned in section 11 (b) he may shorten it to such period as he considers appropriate.

Subsection (2) states that regulations may make provision with respect to the making, and granting, of applications under subsection (1).

Subsection (3) states that regulations under subsection (2) may provide for-

a) the power conferred by subsection (1) to be exercised by a registration authority on behalf of the Registrar General in such classes of case as are prescribed by the regulations;
b) the making of an appeal to the Registrar General against a decision taken by a registration authority in accordance with regulations made by virtue of paragraph (a).

Objection to proposed civil partnership

Section 13 of Part 1 of the Act deals with likely objections to a proposed civil partnership. Subsection (1) states that any person may object to the issue of a proposed civil partnership by giving any registration authority notice of his objection. Subsection (2) states that a notice of objection must-

a) state the objector's place of residence and the grounds for objection, and
b) be signed on or on behalf of the objector.

Subsection (3) states that if a notice of objection is given to a registration authority, it must ensure that the fact that it has been given and the information in it are recorded in the register as soon as possible.

Issue of civil partnership schedule

Section 14 of the Act deals with the issue of a 'schedule' or permission to marry. This is issued after the waiting period and after the registration authority is satisfied that there are no objections to the civil partnership. If the registration authority is not satisfied that the proposed partnership should go ahead then it will not issue a schedule. This could be on the grounds of information provided or on the grounds of an objection, which must be investigated.

Appeal against refusal to issue civil partnership schedule

Section 15 deals with the proposed civil partners right to appeal against refusal to issue a schedule.

Frivolous objections and representations

Section 16 deals with the powers of the registration authority in the event of frivolous objections and representations.

Period during which registration may take place

Section 17 deals with the period during which registration can take place. Subsection (1) states that the proposed civil partners may not register as civil partners of each other on the production of the civil partnership schedule until the waiting period in relation to each notice of proposed civil partnership has expired. Subsection (2) states that subject to subsection (1) under the standard procedure, they may register as civil partners by signing the civil partnership schedule at any time during the applicable period.

Subsection (3) states that if they do not register as civil partners by signing the civil partnership schedule before the end of the applicable period-

a) the notices of proposed civil partnership and the civil partnership schedule are void, and

b) no civil partnership registrar may officiate at the signing of the civil partnership schedule by them.

Subsection (4) states that the applicable period, in relation to two people registering as civil partners of each other, is the period of 12 months beginning with-

a) the day on which notices of proposed civil partnership are recorded, or

b) if the notices are not recorded on the same day, the earlier of those days.

Housebound persons

Section 18 deals with housebound persons. Subsection (1) of section 18 states that this section applies if two people wish to register as civil partners of each other at the place where one of them is housebound.

Subsection (2) states that a person is housebound at any place if, in relation to that person, a statement is made by a registered medical practitioner that, in his opinion-

a) because of illness or disability, that person ought not to move or be moved from the place where he is at the time when the statement is made, and

b) it is likely to be the case for the next three months that because of the illness or disability that person ought not to move or be moved from that place.

Subsection (3) states that the procedure under which the two people concerned may register as civil partners of each other is the same as the standard procedure except that-

a) each notice of proposed civil partnership must be accompanied by a statement under subsection (2) ("a medical statement"), which must have been made not more than 14 days before the day on which the notice is recorded,

b) the fact that the registration authority to whom the notice is given has received the medical statement must be recorded in the register, and

c) the applicable period (for the purposes of section 17) is the period of 3 months beginning with-

(i)   the day on which the notices of proposed civil partnership are recorded, or

(ii)   if the notices are not recorded on the same day, the earlier of those days.

Subsection (4) states that a medical statement must contain such information and must be made in such a manner as may be prescribed by regulations.

Subsection (5) states that a medical statement may not be made in relation to a person who is detained as described in section 19 (2).

Subsection (6) states that for the purposes of this chapter, a person in relation to whom a medical statement is made is to be treated, if he would not otherwise be treated, as resident and usually resident at the place where he is for the time being.

Detained persons

Section 19 deals with detained persons. Subsection (1) states that this section applies if two people wish to register as civil partners of each other at the place where one of them is detained.

Subsection (2) defines "detained" as-

a) as patient in a hospital (but otherwise than by virtue of section 2, 4, 5, 35 or 136 of the Mental Health Act 1983 (c.20) (short term detentions), or

b) in a prison or other place to which the Prison Act 1952 (c.52) applies.

Subsection (3) states that the procedure under which the two people concerned may register as civil partners of each other is the same as the standard procedure, except that-

a) each notice of proposed civil partnership must be accompanied by a supporting statement, which must have been made not more than 21 days before the day on which the notice is recorded,
b) the fact that the registration authority that the notice is given has received the supporting statement must be recorded in the register ,and
c) the applicable period (for the purposes of section 17) is the period of 3 months beginning with-

(i) the day on which the notices of proposed civil partnership are recorded, or
(ii) if the notices are not recorded on the same day, the earlier of those days.

Subsection (4) states that a supporting statement, in relation to a detained person, is a statement made by the responsible authority which-

a) identifies the establishment where the person is detained, and
b) states that the responsible authority has no objection to that establishment being specified in a notice of proposed civil partnership as the place at which the person is to register as a civil partner.

Subsection (5) states that a supporting statement must contain such information and must be made in such a manner as may be prescribed by regulations.

Subsection (6) defines "the responsible authority as-

a) if the person is detained in a hospital, the hospital's managers,
b) if the person is detained in a prison or other place to which the 1952 Act applies, the governor or other officer for the time being in charge of that prison or other place.

Subsection (7) defines "patient" and "hospital" as having the same meaning as in Part 2 of the 1983 Act and "managers" in relation to a hospital, has the same meaning as in section 145(1) of the 1983 Act.

Subsection (8) states that for the purposes of this Chapter, a detained person is to be treated, if he would not be otherwise so treated, as resident and usually resident at the place where he is for the time being.

Modified procedures for certain non- residents
Section 20 deals with modified procedures for certain non- residents. Subsection (1) states that subsection (5) applies in the following 3 cases.

Subsection (2) is where two people wish to register as civil partners of each other in England and Wales and one of them (A) resides in Scotland and the other in England or Wales (B)

Subsection (3) is where two people wish to register as civil partners of each other in England and Wales and one of them (A) resides in Northern Ireland and the other (B) resides in England or Wales;

Subsection (4) is where two people wish to register as civil partners of each other in England and Wales and one of them (A) is a member of Her Majesty's armed forces who is serving outside the United Kingdom and the other (B) resides in England and Wales.

Subsection (5) states that for the purposes of the standard procedure, the procedure for house-bound persons and the procedure for detained persons-

a) A is not required to give a notice of proposed civil partnership under this chapter;

b) B may give a notice of proposed civil partnership and make the necessary declaration without regard to the requirement that would otherwise apply that A must reside in England or Wales;

c) The waiting period is calculated by reference to the day on which B's notice is recorded;

d) The civil partnership schedule is not to be issued by a registration authority unless A or B produces to that registration authority a certificate of no impediment issued to A under the relevant provision;

e) The applicable period is calculated by reference to the day on which B's notice is recorded and, where the standard procedure is used in the first and second cases, is the period of 3 months beginning with that day;

f) Section 31 applies as if in subsections (1)(a) and (2)(c) for "each notice" there were substituted "B's notice".

Subsection (6) states that the "relevant provision" means-

a) if A resides in Scotland, section 97;

b) if A resides in Northern Ireland, section 150;

c) if A is a member of Her Majesty's armed forces who is serving outside the United Kingdom, section 239.

Subsection (7) states that "Her Majesty's forces" has the same meaning as in the Army Act 1955 (3 and 4 Eliz. 2 c.18).

The special procedure
Notice of proposed civil partnership

Section 21 of the Act deals with the special procedure and notices of proposed civil partnership. Subsection (1) of section 21 states that for two people to register as civil partners of each other under the special procedure, one of them must-

a) give a notice of proposed civil partnership to the registration authority for the area in which it is proposed that the registration takes place, and

b) comply with any requirement made under section 22.

Subsection (2) states that the notice must contain such information as may be prescribed by regulations.

Subsection (3) states that subsections (3) to (6) of section 8 (necessary declarations etc.) apart from paragraph (b) of subsection (4), apply for the purposes of this section as they apply for purposes of that section.

Evidence to be produced

Section 22 deals with evidence to be produced under the special procedure. Subsection (1) of section 22 states that the person giving a notice of proposed civil procedure must produce to the authority such evidence as the Registrar General may require to satisfy him-

a) that there is no lawful impediment to the formation of the civil partnership,

b) that the conditions in subsection (2) are met, and

c) that there is sufficient reason why a licence should be granted.

Subsection (2) states that the conditions are that one of the proposed civil partners-

a) is seriously ill and not expected to recover, and

b) understands the nature and purport of signing a Registrar General's licence.

Subsection (3) states that the certificate of a registered medical practitioner is sufficient evidence of any or all of the matters referred to in subsection (2).

Application to be reported to Registrar General

Section 24 deals with applications which must be reported to the Registrar General. On receiving notice of proposed civil partnership under section 21 and any evidence under section 22, the registration authority must-

a) inform the Registrar General, and
b) comply with any directions the Registrar General may give for verifying the evidence given.

Objection to issue of Registrar General's notice

Section 24 deals with objections. Subsection (1) of section 24 states that any person may object to the Registrar General giving authority for the issue of his licence by giving the Registrar General or any registration authority notice of his objection.

Subsection (2) states that a notice of objection must-

a) state the objector's place of residence and the ground of objection, and
b) be signed on or on behalf of the objector.

Subsection (3) states that if a notice of objection is given to a registration authority, it must ensure that the fact that it has been given and the information in it are recorded in the register as soon as possible.

Issue of Registrar General's notice

Section 25 deals with the issue of notice. Subsection (1) of section 25 states that this section applies where a notice of proposed civil partnership is given to a registration authority under section 21.

Subsection (2) states that the registration authority may issue a Registrar General's licence if, and only if, given authority to do so by the Registrar General.

Subsection (3) states that the Registrar General-

a) may not give his authority unless he is satisfied that one of the proposed civil partners is seriously ill and not expected to recover, but

b) if so satisfied, must give his authority unless a lawful impediment to the issue of his licence has been shown to his satisfaction to exist.

Subsection (4) states that a licence under this section must state that it is issued on the authority of the Registrar General.

Subsection (5) states that regulations may (subject to subsection (4)) make provision as to the contents of a licence under this section.

Subsection (6) states that if an objection has been made to the Registrar General giving authority for the issue of his licence, he is not to give that authority until-

a) he has investigated the objection and decided whether it ought to obstruct the issue of his licence, or

b) the objection has been withdrawn by the person who made it.

Subsection (7) states that any decision of the Registrar General under subsection (6)(a) is final.

Frivolous objections: liability for costs

Section 26 deals with frivolous objections. Subsection (1) states that this section applies if-

a) a person objects to the Registrar General giving authority for the issue of his licence, but

b) the Registrar General declares that the grounds on which the objection is made arc frivolous and ought not to obstruct the issue of his licence.

Subsection (2) states that the person who made the objection is liable for-

a) any costs of the proceedings before the Registrar General, and
b) damages recoverable by the proposed civil partner to whom the objection relates.

Subsection (3) states that for the purpose of enabling any person to recover any such costs and damages, a copy of a declaration of the Registrar General purporting to be sealed with the seal of the General Register Office is evidence that the Registrar General has made the declaration.

Period during which registration may take place

Section 27 deals with the period during which registration may take place. Subsection (1) of section 27 states that if a Registrar General's licence has been issued under section 25, the proposed civil partners may register as civil partners by signing it at any time within 1 month from the day on which the notice of proposed civil partnership was given.

Subsection (2) states that if they do not register as civil partners by signing the licence within the 1 month period-

a) the notice of proposed civil partnership and the licence are void, and
b) no civil partnership registrar may officiate at the signing of the licence by them.

Supplementary

Registration authorities

Section 28 deals with definitions of registration authority. In this chapter "registration authority" means-

a) in relation to England, a county council, the council of any district comprised in an area for which there is no county council, a London borough council, the Common Council of the City of London or the Council of the Isles of Scilly;

b) in relation to Wales, a county council or a county borough council.

Civil partnership registrars

Section 29 deals with civil partnership registrars. Subsection (1) states that a civil partnership registrar is an individual who is designated by a registration authority as a civil partnership registrar for its area.

Subsection (2) states that it is the duty of each registration authority to ensure that there is a sufficient number of civil partnership registrars for its area to carry out in that area the functions of civil partnership registrars.

Subsection (3) states that each registration authority must inform the registrar general as soon as is practicable-

a) of any designation it has made of a person as a civil partnership registrar, and

b) the ending of any such designation.

Subsection (4) states that the Registrar General must make available to the public a list-

a) of civil partnership registrars, and

b) of the registration authorities for which they are designated to act.

The Registrar General and the register

Section 30 deals with the Registrar General. Subsection (1) of section 30 states that in this chapter the "Registrar General" means the Registrar General for England and Wales.

Subsection (2) states that the Registrar General must provide a system for keeping any records that relate to civil partnerships and are required by this Chapter to be made.

Subsection (3) states that the system may, in particular, enable those records to be kept together with other records kept by the Registrar General.

Subsection (4) states that in this Chapter "the register" means the system for keeping records provided under subsection (2).

Offences relating to civil partnership schedule

Section 31 relates to offences and the civil partnership schedule. Subsection (1) states that a person commits an offence if he issues a civil partnership schedule knowing that he does so-

a) before the waiting period in relation to each notice of proposed civil partnership has expired,
b) after the end of the applicable period, and
c) at a time when its issue has been forbidden under Schedule 2 by a person entitled to forbid its issue.

Subsection (2) states that a person commits an offence if, in his actual or purported capacity as a civil partnership registrar, he officiates at the signing of a civil partnership schedule by proposed civil partners knowing that he does so-

a) at a place other than the place specified in the notices of proposed civil partnership and the civil partnership schedule,
b) in the absence of a civil partnership registrar,
c) before the waiting period in relation to each notice of proposed civil partnership has expired, or
d) even though the civil partnership is void under section 49 (b) or (c).

Subsection (3) states that a person guilty of an offence under subsection (1) or (2) is liable on conviction on indictment to imprisonment for a term not exceeding 5 years or to a fine (or both).

Subsection (4) states that a prosecution under this section may not be commenced more than 3 years after the commission of the offence.

Offences relating to Registrar General's notice

Section 32 deals with offences relating to the Registrar General's licences. Subsection (1) states that a person commits an offence if-

a) he gives information by way of evidence in response to a requirement under s 22(1), knowing that the information is false;
b) he gives a certificate as provided for by section 22(3) knowing that the certificate is false;

Subsection (2) states that a person commits an offence if, in his actual or purported capacity as a civil partnership registrar, he officiates at the signing of a Registrar General's licence by proposed civil partners knowing that he does so-

a) at a place other than the place specified in the licence,
b) in the absence of a civil partnership registrar,
c) after the end of 1 month from the day on which the notice of proposed civil partnership was given, or
d) even though the civil partnership is void under section 49 (b) or (c).

Subsection (3) states that a person guilty of an offence under subsection (1) or (2) is liable-

a) on conviction on indictment, to imprisonment not exceeding 3 years or to a fine or both,

b)   on summary conviction, to a fine not exceeding the statutory maximum.

Subsection (4) states that a prosecution under this section may not be commenced more than 3 years after the commission of the offence.

Offences relating to the recording of a civil partnership

Section 33 deals with offences relating to the recording of a civil partnership. Subsection (1) states that a civil partnership registrar commits an offence if he refuses or fails to comply with the provisions of this Chapter or of any regulations made under section 36.

Subsection (2) states that a civil partnership registrar guilty of an offence under subsection (1) is liable-

a)   on conviction on indictment, to imprisonment for a term not exceeding 2 years or to a fine or both;

b)   on summary conviction, to a fine not exceeding the statutory maximum;

and on conviction shall cease to be a civil partnership registrar.

Subsection (3) states that a person commits an offence if-

a)   under arrangements made by a registration authority for the purposes of section 2 (4) , he is under a duty to record information required to be recorded under section 2 (4), but

b)   he refuses or without reasonable cause omits to do so.

Subsection (4) states that a person guilty of an offence under subsection (3) is liable on summary conviction to a fine not exceeding level 3 on the standard scale.

Subsection (5) states that a person commits an offence if he records in the register information relating to the formation of a civil partnership by the signing of a civil partnership schedule, knowing that the civil partnership is void under section 49 (b) or (c).

Subsection (6) states that a person guilty of an offence under subsection (5) is liable on conviction or indictment, to imprisonment for a term not exceeding 5 years or to a fine or both.

Subsection (7) states that a person commits an offence if he records in the register information relating to the formation of a civil partnership by the signing of a Registrar General's licence, knowing that the civil partnership is void under section 49(b) or (c).

Subsection (8) states that a person guilty of an offence under subsection (7) is liable-

a) on conviction on indictment, to imprisonment for a term not exceeding three years or to a fine or both;
b) on summary conviction, to a fine not exceeding the statutory maximum.

Subsection (9) states that a prosecution under subsection (5) or (7) may not be commenced more than 3 years after the commission of the offence.

Fees
Section 34 deals with fees. See introduction for a breakdown of fees payable. Section 34 outlines the powers of the Chancellor of the Exchequer to set fees and the powers of the Registrar General to remit fees in cases of hardship. Section 35 and 36 deal with powers to assimilate provisions relating to civil registration (35) and regulations and orders (36).

****

Chapter 4.

Dissolution of Civil Partnerships

Dissolution of a Civil Partnership, Nullity and Other Proceedings.

Paragraph 34 of the Marriage (Same Sex Persons) Act 2013 amends the provisions in the Civil partnership Act, which set out how a civil partnership can be ended. The amendment provides that, in addition to death, dissolution and annulment, a civil partnership ends if it is converted into a marriage under section 9 of the Act.

Section 37 of Chapter 2 of the Civil Partnerships Act 2004 deals with the ending of a civil partnership, either through dissolution or nullity or other.

As with marriage, problems may arise and partners to a civil partnership may wish to terminate the union. Likewise, the union may not, for some reason, be legal and may be annulled. Later chapters deal with economic and other matters which will arise after dissolution.

By virtue of Section 37 the court may:

a) make a dissolution order which dissolves a civil partnership on the ground that it has broken down irretrievably;

b) make a nullity order which annuls a civil partnership which is void or voidable;

c) make a presumption of death order which dissolves a civil partnership on the ground that one of the civil partners is presumed to be dead;

d) make a separation order which provides for the separation of the civil partners.

Further, every dissolution, nullity or presumption of death order:

a) is, in the first instance, a conditional order and;
b) may not be made final before the end of the prescribed period (see below).

A nullity order made where a civil partnership is voidable annuls the civil partnership only as respects any time after the order, and the civil partnership is to be treated (despite the order) as if it had existed up to that time.

Courts can be the High Court or, if the County Court has jurisdiction by virtue of Part 5 of the Matrimonial and Family Proceedings Act 1984, a county court.

The period before conditional orders can be made final

Section 38 of the Act states that the prescribed period referred to above is:

a) 6 weeks from the making of the conditional order, or
b) if the 6-week period would end on a day on which the office or the registry dealing with the case is closed, the period of 6 weeks extended to the first day on which the offices are next open.

This prescribed period can be replaced with a different definition by the Lord Chancellor. Six months, however, will be the maximum prescribed period. In a particular case, the court dealing with the case can shorten the prescribed period. Any instrument carrying such an order is subject to annulment by a resolution of either houses of parliament.

Intervention of the Queen's proctor

This section, 39, will apply if an application has been made for a dissolution, nullity or presumption of death order. The court may, if it thinks fit, direct all necessary papers are to be sent to the Queen's proctor who must under the directions of the Attorney General instruct counsel to argue before the court any question in relation to the matter which the court considers it necessary or expedient to have fully argued.

If any person at any time either during the progress of the proceedings or before the conditional order is made final gives information to the Queen's Proctor on any matter material to the due decision of the case, the Queen's proctor may take such steps as the Attorney general considers necessary or expedient.

If the Queen's Proctor does intervene the courts can award costs of such an intervention against appropriate parties.

Proceedings before an order has been made final

Section 40 deals with any proceedings or events prior to an order being made final. The section applies if a conditional order has been made and the Queen's proctor or any other person who has not been party to a proceedings in which an order was made, shows cause why the order should not be made final on the ground that material facts have not been brought before the court. The section also applies if:

a) a conditional order has been made,
b) three months have elapsed since the earliest date on which an application could have been made for the order to be made final,
c) no such application has been made by the civil partner who applied for the conditional order, and
d) the other civil partner makes an application to the court under this section.

The court may:
a) make the order final
b) rescind the order
c) require further enquiry
d) other wise deal with the case as it thinks fit.

Time bar on application for dissolution orders

Section 41 of the Act deals with time limits on applications for orders. No application for a dissolution order may be made to the court before the end of the period of one year from the formation of the civil partnership. Nothing in the section prevents an application being made which includes matters that happened before the end of the 1-year period.

Attempts at reconciliation of civil partners

Section 42 of the Act applies where an application has been made for a dissolution or separation order. The rules of the court must make provision for requiring the solicitor acting for the applicant to certify whether he or she has discussed with the applicant the possibility of a reconciliation with the civil partner and given the applicant the name and address of persons qualified to act in helping to effect a reconciliation of the civil partners. If at any stage of the proceedings it seems to the court that there is a reasonable possibility of a reconciliation between the civil partners, the court may adjourn the proceedings for such period as it thinks fit to enable attempts to be made to effect a reconciliation between them.

Consideration by the court of any agreements or arrangements

Section 43 applies in cases where proceedings for a dissolution or separation order is contemplated or have begun and an agreement or arrangement is made or proposed to be made between the civil partners which relates to, arises out of, or is connected with, the proceedings. The civil partners, or either of them, can refer the arrangement to court and the court will consider the arrangement.

Dissolution of a civil partnership which has broken down irretrievably

Subject to section 41, under section 44 of the Act, an application for a dissolution order may be made to the court by either civil partner on the ground that the civil partnership has broken down irretrievably.

On an application for a dissolution order the court must inquire, as far as it reasonably can, into:

a) the facts alleged by the applicant, and
b) the facts alleged by the respondent.

The court hearing an application for a dissolution order must not hold that the civil partnership has broken down irretrievably unless the applicant satisfies the court of one or more of the facts described below (sub section 5(a), (b), (c) or (d)). If the court is satisfied of any of the facts described below it must make a dissolution order unless it is satisfied on all the evidence that the partnership has not broken down irretrievably.

The facts laid out in subsection 5(a) (b) (c) or (d) of section 41 of the act are:

a) that the respondent has behaved in such a way that the applicant cannot reasonably be expected to live with the respondent;

b) that:

   (i) the applicant and the respondent have lived apart for a continuous period of at least 2 years immediately preceding the making of the application (2 years separation), and

   (ii) the respondent consents to a dissolution order being made;

c) that the applicant and the respondent have lived apart for a continuous period of at least 5 years immediately preceding the making of the application (5 years separation);

d) that the respondent has deserted the applicant for a continuous period of at least 2 years immediately preceding the making of the application.

Supplemental provisions as to facts raising presumption of breakdown

Section 45 of the Act relates to additional facts that effect the making of an order for a dissolution of a civil partnership.

a) in any proceedings for a dissolution order the applicant alleges, in reliance on s44 (5)(a) that the respondent has behaved in such a way that the applicant cannot reasonably be expected to live with the respondent, but

b) after the date of the occurrence of the final incident relied on by the applicant and held by the court to support his allegation, the applicant and the respondent have lived together for a period (or period) which does not, or which taken together do not, exceed 6 months.

The fact that the applicant and respondent have lived together as mentioned in subsection (b) must be disregarded in determining, for the purposes of 44(5)(b) whether the applicant cannot reasonably be expected to live with the respondent.

Section 45 states that the rules of the court must make provision for the purpose of ensuring that the respondent has been given such information as will enable him or her to understand the consequences to him of consenting to the making of the order and the steps which he or she must take to indicate consent.

For the purposes of section 44(5)(d) the court may treat a period of desertion as having continued at a time when the deserting partner was incapable of continuing the necessary intention, if the evidence before the court is such that, had he not been so incapable, the court would have inferred that the desertion would have continued at that time.

In considering for the purposes of section 44(5) whether the period for which the civil partners have lived apart or the period for which the respondent has deserted the applicant has been continuous, no account is to be taken of :

a) any one period not exceeding 6 months, or
b) any two or more periods no exceeding 6 months in all, during which the civil partners resumed living with each other.

But no period during which the civil partners have lived with each other counts as part of the period during which the civil partners have lived apart as part of the period of desertion.

Dissolution order not precluded by previous separation order etc

Section 46 of the Act states that subsections (1) (2) and (3) apply if any of the following orders has been made in relation to a civil partnership:

a) a separation order;
b) an order under schedule 6 to the Act (financial relief in magistrates courts etc)
c) an order under section 33 of the Family Law Act 1966 (c.27) (occupation orders)
d) an order under section 37 of the 1996 Act (orders where neither civil partner entitled to share the home)

Subsection (2) states that nothing prevents either civil partner from applying for a dissolution order or the court from making a dissolution order on the same facts, or substantially the same facts, as those proved in support of the making of the order referred to above.

Subsection (3) section 46 states that on the application for the dissolution order the court may treat the order referred to above as sufficient proof of any desertion or other fact by reference to which it was made but must not make the dissolution order without receiving evidence from the applicant.

Subsection (4) states that if the application for the dissolution order follows a separation order or any order requiring the civil partners to live apart, and there was a degree of desertion immediately preceding the institution of the proceedings for the separation order, and the civil partners have not resumed living together and the separation order has continuously been in force since it was made, then the period of desertion is to be treated for the purposes of the application of the dissolution order as if it had immediately preceded the making of the application.

Subsection (5) states that for the purposes of s (44)(5)(d) the court may treat as a period during which the respondent has deserted the applicant any period during which there was in force:

a) an injunction granted by the high court or a county court which excludes the respondent from the civil partnership home, or

b) an order under section 33 or 37 of the 1996 Act which prohibits the respondent from occupying a dwelling house in which the applicant and the respondent have or at any time have had, a civil partnership home.

Refusal of dissolution in 5-year separation cases on grounds of grave hardship

Section 47 deals with the opposing of a dissolution order by the respondent. Subsection (1) states that the respondent to an application for a dissolution order in which the applicant alleges 5 years separation may oppose the making of the order on the grounds that:

a) the dissolution of the civil partnership will result in grave or other financial hardship to him/her, and,

b) it would in all the circumstances be wrong to dissolve the civil partnership.

Subsection (2) states that subsection (3) (below) applies if:

a) the making of a dissolution order is opposed under this section,

b) the court finds that the applicant is entitled to rely in support of his application on the fact of 5 years separation and makes no such finding as to any other fact mentioned in section 44(5), and

c) apart from this section, the court would make a dissolution order.

Subsection 3 states that the court must consider all the circumstances, including the conduct of the civil partners and the interests of the civil partners and any of the children or other persons concerned, and if it is of the opinion that the ground mentioned in subsection 1 is made out, dismiss the application for the dissolution order.

Subsection (4) further defines 'hardship' as including the loss of the chance of acquiring any benefit which the respondent might acquire if the civil partnership were not dissolved.

Proceedings before order made final: protection for respondent in separation cases

Section 48 of the Act deals with the protection of the respondent in separation cases. Subsection (1) states that the court may, on application made by the respondent, rescind a conditional dissolution order if:

a) it made the order on the basis of a finding that the applicant was entitled to rely on the fact of 2 years separation coupled with the respondents consent to a dissolution order being made,

b) it made no such finding as to any other fact mentioned in section 44(5) and

c) it is satisfied that the applicant misled the respondent (whether intentionally or unintentionally) about any matter which the respondent took into account when deciding to give his consent.

Subsection 2 of section 48 states that subsections (3) to (5) apply if:

a) the respondent to an application for a dissolution order in which the applicant alleged:

   (i)   2 years separation coupled with the respondent's consent to a dissolution order being made, or

   (ii) 5 years separation

has applied to the court for consideration under subsection (3) of his financial position after the dissolution of the civil partnership, and

b) the court:

   (i)   has made a conditional dissolution order on the basis of a finding that the applicant was entitled to rely in support of his application on the fact of 2 years or 5 years separation, and

   (ii) has made no such finding as to any other fact mentioned in section 44(5).

Subsection (3) of section 48 states that the court hearing an application by the respondent under subsection (2) must consider all the circumstances, including:

a) the health, age, conduct, earning capacity, financial resources and financial obligations of each of the parties, and

b) the financial position of the respondent as, having regard to the dissolution it is likely to be after the death of the applicant should the applicant die first.

Subsection (4) states that, subject to subsection (5) the court must not make an order final unless it is satisfied that:

a) the applicant should not be required to make any financial provision for the respondent, or

b) the financial provision made by the applicant for the respondent is-

    (i)   fair and reasonable

    (ii)   the best that can be made in the circumstances.

Subsection (5) states that the court may if it thinks fit make the order final if:

a) it appears that there are circumstances making it desirable that the order should be made final without delay, and
b) it has obtained a satisfactory undertaking from the applicant that he will make such financial provision for the respondent as it may approve.

Nullity
Grounds on which a civil partnership is void

Section 49 deals with nullity of a civil partnership. Nullity effectively means a void civil partnership.

Where two people register as civil partners of each other in England and Wales, the civil partnership is void if:

a) at the time when they do so, they are not eligible to register as civil partners under Chapter 1,
b) at the time when they do so they both know-

    (i)   that the notice of proposed civil partnership has not been given,

    (ii)   that the civil partnership document has not been duly issued,

    (iii)   that the civil partnership document is void

    (iv)   that the place of registration is a place other than that specified in the notices (or notice) of proposed civil partnership and the civil partnership document, or

(v)   that a civil partnership registrar is not present, or

c) the civil partnership document is void under paragraph 6 (5) of Schedule 2 to the Act (civil partnership between child and another person forbidden). .

Grounds on which civil partnership is voidable

Section 50 of the Act deals with grounds on which a civil partnership can be voided. Subsection (1) states that where two people register as civil partners of each other in England and Wales, the civil partnership is voidable if:

a) either of them did not validly consent to its formation (whether as a result of duress, mistake, unsoundness of mind or otherwise)

b) at the time of its formation either of them, though capable of giving a valid consent, was suffering, whether continuously or intermittently, from mental disorder of such a kind or to such an extent as to be unfitted for civil partnership;

c) at the time of its formation, the respondent was pregnant by some person other than the applicant;

d) an interim gender recognition certificate under the Gender Recognition Act 2004 (c.7) has, after the time of its formation, been issued to either civil partner;

e) the respondent is a person whose gender at the time of its formation had become the acquired gender under the 2004 Act.

(2) In this section and section 51 'mental disorder' has the same meaning as in the Mental Health Act 1983 (c.20).

Bars to relief where civil partnership is voidable

Section 51 deals with relief in relation to making a nullity order. Subsection (1) of section 51 states that the court must not make a nullity order on the ground that a civil partnership is voidable if the respondent satisfies the court:

a) that the applicant, with knowledge that it was open to him to obtain a nullity order, conducted himself in relation to the respondent in such a way as to lead the respondent reasonably to believe that he would not seek to do so, and

b) that it would be unjust to the respondent to make the order.

Subsection 2 states that, without prejudice to subsection (1) the court must not make a nullity order by virtue of section 50(1)(a),(b)(C) or(e) unless-

a) it is satisfied that proceedings were instituted within 3 years from the date of the formation of the civil partnership, or

b) leave for the institution of proceedings after the end of that 3 year period has been granted under subsection (3).

Subsection (3) states that a judge of the court may, on an application made to him, grant leave for the intention of proceedings if he:

a) is satisfied that the applicant has at some time during the three year period suffered from mental disorder, and

b) considers that in all the circumstances of the case it would be just to grant leave for the institution of the proceedings.

Subsection (4) states that an application for leave under subsection (3) may be made after the end of the 3 year period.

Subsection (5) states that, without prejudice to subsection (1) the court must not make a nullity order by virtue of section 50(1)(d) unless it is satisfied that proceedings were instituted within the period of 6 months from the date of issue of the interim gender recognition certificate.

Subsection (6) states that, without prejudice to subsection (1) and (2) the court must not make a nullity order by virtue of section 50(1)(c) or

(e) unless it is satisfied that the applicant was at the time of the formation of the civil partnership ignorant of the facts alleged.

Proof of certain matters not necessary to validity of civil partnership

Section 52, subsection (1) of the Act states that where two people have registered as civil partners of each other in England and Wales, it is not necessary in support of the civil partnership to give any proof:

a) that any person whose consent to the civil partnership was required under section 4 (parental etc. consent) had given his consent, or

b) that the civil partnership registrar was designated as such by the registration authority in whose area the registration took place;

and no evidence is to be given to prove the contrary in any proceedings touching the validity of the civil partnership.

Power to validate civil partnership

Section 53 of the Act deals with powers to validate a civil partnership. Subsection (1) of section 53 states that where two people have registered as civil partners of each other in England and Wales, the Lord Chancellor may by order validate the civil partnership if it appears to him that it is or may be void under section 49(b).

Subsection (2) states that an order under subsection (1) may include provisions for relieving a person from any liability under section 31(2) 32(2) 0r 33(5) or (7).

Subsection (3) states that the draft of an order under subsection (1) must be advertised, in such manner as the Lord Chancellor thinks fit, not less than one month before the order is made.

Subsection (4) states that the Lord Chancellor must:

a) consider all objections to the order sent to him in writing during that month, and

b) if it appears to him necessary, direct a local enquiry into the validity of any such objections.

Subsection (5) states that an order under subsection (1) is subject to special parliamentary procedure.

Validity of civil partnerships registered outside England and Wales

Section 54 of the Act deals with civil partnerships registered outside England and Wales. Subsection (1) of section 54 states that where two people register as civil partners of each other in Scotland, the civil partnership is-

a) void, if it would be void in Scotland under section 123, and

b) voidable, if the circumstances fall within section 50(1)(d).

Subsection (2) states that where two people register as civil partners of each other in Northern Ireland, the civil partnership is-

a) void, if it would be void in Northern Ireland under section 173, and

b) voidable, if circumstances fall within any paragraph of section 50(1).

Subsection (3) states that subsection (4) below applies where two people register as civil partners of each other under an order in Council under-

a) section 210 (registration at British consulates etc,) or

b) section 211 (registration by armed forces personnel),

(the 'relevant section')

Subsection (4) states that the civil partnership is-

a) void, if-

    (i)   the condition in subsection (2) (a) 0r (b) of the relevant section is not met, or

    (ii)   a requirement prescribed for the purposes of this paragraph by an Order in Council under the relevant section is not complied with, and

(b) voidable if,

    (i)   the appropriate part of the United Kingdom is England and Wales or Northern Ireland and the circumstances fall within any paragraph of section 50(1), or

    (ii)   the appropriate part of the United Kingdom is Scotland and the circumstances fall within section 50(1)(d).

Subsection (5) states that the appropriate part of the United kingdom is the part by reference to which the condition in subsection (2)(b) of the relevant section is met.

Subsection (6) states that subsections (7) and (8) below apply where two people have registered an apparent or alleged overseas relationship.

(7) The civil partnership is void if-

a) the relationship is not an overseas relationship, or
b) (even though the relationship is an overseas relationship) the parties are not treated under chapter 2 of part 5 as having formed a civil partnership.

(8) The civil partnership is voidable if-

a) the overseas relationship is voidable under section 50(1)(d), or

b) the circumstances fall within section 50(1)(d), or

c) where either of the parties was domiciled in England and Wales or Northern Ireland at the time when the overseas relationship was registered, the circumstances fall within section 50(1)(a)(b)(c)or(e)

Presumption of death orders

Section 55 of the Act deals with presumption of death orders. Subsection (1) states that the court may, on an application made by a civil partner, make a presumption of death order if it is satisfied that reasonable grounds exist for supposing that the other civil partner is dead.

Subsection (2) states that, in any proceedings under this section the fact that:

a) for a period of 7 years or more the civil partner has been continually absent from the applicant, and

b) the applicant has no reason to believe that the other civil partner has been living within that time.

is evidence that the other civil partner is dead until the contrary is proved.

Separation orders

Section 56 deals with separation orders. Subsection (1) of section 56 states that an application for a separation order may be made to the court by either civil partner on the ground that any such fact as is mentioned in section 44(5)(a),(b),(c) or (d) exists.

Subsection (2) states that on an application for a separation order the court must inquire, so far as it reasonably can, into-

a) the facts alleged by the applicant, and

b) any facts alleged by the respondent,

but whether the civil partnership has broken down irretrievably is irrelevant.

Subsection (3) states that, if the court is satisfied on the evidence of any such fact as mentioned in section 44(5)(a),(b),(c) or (d) it must, subject to section 63, make a separation order.

Subsection (4) states that section 45 (supplemental provisions as to facts raising presumption of breakdown) applies for the purposes of an application for a separation order alleging any such fact as it applies in relation to an application for a dissolution order alleging that fact.

Effect of a separation order
Section 57 deals with the effect of a separation order. If either civil partner dies intestate as respects all or any of his or her real or personal property while a separation order is in force and the separation is continuing, the property as respects which he or she died intestate devolves as if the other civil partner had then been dead.

Declarations
Section 58 of the Act deals with declarations. Subsection (1) of section 58 states that any person may apply to the high court or a county court for one or more of the following declarations in relation to a civil partnership specified in the application:

a) a declaration that the civil partnership was at its inception a valid civil partnership;

b) a declaration that the civil partnership subsisted on a date specified in the application;

c) a declaration that the civil partnership did not subsist on a date so specified;

d) a declaration that the validity of a dissolution, annulment or legal separation obtained outside England and Wales in respect of the civil partnership is entitled to recognition in England and Wales;

e)   a declaration that the validity of a dissolution, annulment or legal separation so obtained in respect of the civil partnership is not entitled to recognition in England and Wales.

Subsection (2) of section 58 states that where an application under subsection (1) is made to a court by a person other than a civil partner in the civil partnership to which the application relates, the court must refuse to hear the application if it considers that the applicant does not have a sufficient interest in the determination of that application.

General provisions as to making and effect of declarations

Section 59 of the Act deals with general provisions relating to the making and effect of declarations. Subsection (1) of section 59 states that where on an application for a declaration under section 58 the truth of the proposition to be declared is proved to the satisfaction of the court, the court must make the declaration unless to do so would be manifestly contrary to public policy.

Subsection (2) states that ay declaration under section 58 binds her majesty and all other persons.

Subsection (3) states that the court, on the dismissal of an application for a declaration under section 58, may not make any declaration for which an application has not been made.

Subsection (4) states that no declaration which may be applied for under section 58 may be made otherwise than under section 58 by any court.

Subsection (5) states that no declaration may be made by any court, whether under section 58 or otherwise, that a civil partnership was, at its inception void.

Subsection (6) states that nothing in this section affects the powers of any court to make a nullity order in respect of a civil partnership.

The Attorney General and proceedings for declarations

Section 60 of the Act deals with the powers of the Attorney General to intervene with an application under section 58 and also the powers of the court to refer a matter to him or her.

Supplementary provisions as to declarations

Section 61 deals with supplementary provisions relating to declarations. Subsection (1) of section 61 of the Act states that any declaration made under section 68, and any application for such a declaration, must be in the form prescribed by the rules of the court. Subsection (2) states that the rules of the court may make provision as to the information required to be given by any applicant for a declaration under section 58. The rules can also require notice of an application under section 58 to be served on the attorney general and on persons who may be affected by any declaration applied for.

Subsection (3) states that no proceedings under section 58 affect any final judgement or order already pronounced or made by any court of competent jurisdiction. Subsection (4) states that the court hearing an application under section 58 may direct that the whole or part of any proceedings must be heard in private.

Subsection (5) states that an application for a direction under subsection (4) must be heard in private unless the court other wise directs.

General provisions under Chapter two of the Act

Sections 62 63 and 64 deal with general provisions. Section 62 deals with relief for respondents in dissolution proceedings, Section 63 deals with restrictions on making of orders affecting children (the court must consider the effects of any dissolution, nullity or separation orders on the welfare of children). Subsection (1) of section 63 states that in any proceedings for a dissolution, nullity or separation order, the court must consider:

a) whether there are any children of the family to whom this section applies, and

b) if thee are any such children, whether (in the light of the arrangements which have been, or are proposed to be, made for their upbringing and welfare) it should exercise any of its powers under the Children Act 1989 (c.41) with respect to any of them.

Subsection (2) states that, if, in the case of any child to whom this section applies, it appears to the court that-

a) the circumstances of the case require it, or are likely to require it, to exercise any of its powers under the 1989 Act with respect to any such child,

b) it is not in the position to exercise the power or (as the case may be) those powers without giving further consideration to the case, and

c) there are exceptional circumstances which make it desirable in the interests of the child that the court should give a direction under this section, it may direct that the order is not to be made final, or (in the case of a separation order) is not to be made, until the court orders otherwise.

Subsection (3) states that this section applies to:

a) any child of the family who has not reached 16 at the date when the court considers the case in accordance with the requirements of this section, and

b) any child of the family who has reached 16 at that date and in relation to whom the court directs that this section shall apply.

Section 64 deals with general rules concerning parties to proceedings under Chapter 2 of the act.

****

Chapter 5.

Property and Financial Arrangements

Property and Financial Arrangements

Section 65 of Chapter 3 of the 2004 Civil Partnerships Act deals with property and financial arrangements in relation to entitlements generally and the event of a dissolution and ending of a partnership.

Subsection (1) of section 65 applies if:

a) a civil partner contributes in money or money's worth to the improvement of real or personal property in which or in the proceeds of sale of which either or both of the civil partners has or have a beneficial interest, and

b) the contribution is of a substantial nature.

Subsection (2) states that the contributing partner is to be treated as having acquired by virtue of the contribution a share or an enlarged share (as the case may be) in the beneficial interest of such an extent:

a) as may have been then agreed, or
b) in default of such agreement, as may seem in all the circumstances just to any court before which the question of the existence or extent of the beneficial interest of either civil partners arises (whether in proceedings between them or in any other proceedings)

Subsection (3) states that subsection (2) is subject to any agreement (express or implied) between the civil partners to the contrary.

Disputes between civil partners about property

Section 66 of the Act deals with disputes about property. Subsection (1) of section 66 states that in any question between the civil partners in a civil partnership as to title to or possession of property, either civil partner may apply to the High Court or such county court as may be prescribed by rules of court.

Subsection (2) states that on such an application, the court may make such order with respect to the property as it thinks fit (including an order for the sale of the property).

Subsection (3) states that rules of the court made for the purpose of this section may confer jurisdiction on county courts whatever the situation or value of the property in dispute.

Applications under section 66 where property not in possession etc.

Section 67 deals with applications under section 66 where one or other civil partner has property which is in possession of one person only.

Subsection (1) of section 67 states that the right of a civil partner (A) to make an application under section 66 includes the right to make such an application where A claims that the other civil partner (B) has had in his possession or under his control:

a) money to which, or to a share of which, A was beneficially entitled, or
b) property (other than money) to which, or to an interest in which, A was beneficially entitled, and that either the money or other property has ceased to be in B's possession or under B's control or that A does not know whether it is still in B's possession or under B's control.

Subsection (2) states that for the purposes of subsection (1)(a) it does not matter whether A is beneficially entitled to the money or share:

a) because it represents the proceeds of the property to which, or to an interest in which, A was beneficially entitled, or
b) for any other reason.

Subsection (3) states that subsections (4) and (5) below apply if, on such an application being made, the court is satisfied that B:

a) has had in his possession or under his control money or other property as mentioned in subsection (1)(a) or (b), and
b) has not made to A, in respect of that money or other property, such payment or disposition as would have been appropriate in the circumstances.

Subsection (4) states that the power of the court to make orders under section 66 includes power to order B to pay A:

a) in a case falling within subsection (1)(a) such sum in respect of the money to which the application relates, or A's share of it, the court considers appropriate, or
b) in a case falling within subsection (1)(b), such sum in respect of the value of the property to which the application relates, or A's interest in it, as the court considers appropriate.

Subsection (5) states that if it appears to the court that there is any property which:

a) represents the whole or the part of the money or property, and
b) is property in respect of which an order could (apart from this section) have been made under section 66, the court may (either instead of or as well as making an order in accordance with subsection (4) make any order which it could (apart from this section) have made under section 66.

Subsection (6) states that any power of the court which is exercisable on an application under section 66 is exercisable in relation to an application made under that section as extended by that section.

Applications under section 66 by former civil partners

Section 68 of the Act deals with applications by former civil partners. Subsection (1) of section 68 states that this section applies where a civil partnership has been dissolved or annulled. Subsection (2) states that, subject to subsection (3) below, an application may be made under section 66 (including that section as extended by section 67) by either former civil partner despite the dissolution or annulment (and references in those sections to a civil partner are to be read accordingly).

Subsection (3) states that the application must be made within the period of 3 years beginning with the date of the dissolution or annulment.

Actions in tort between civil partners

Section 69 of the Act deals with tortuous actions between civil partners. Subsection (1) of section 69 states that this section applies if an action in tort is brought by one civil partner against the other during the subsistence of the civil partnership.

Subsection (2) states that the court may stay the proceedings if it appears:

a) that no substantial benefit would accrue to either civil partner from the continuation of the proceedings, or
b) that the question or questions in issue could more conveniently be disposed of on an application under section 66.

Subsection (3) states that without prejudice to subsection (2)(b) the court may in such an action-

a) exercise any power which could be exercised on an application under section 66, or
b) give such direction as it thinks fit for the disposal under that section of any question arising in the proceedings.

Assurance policy by civil partner for benefit of other civil partner etc.

Section 70 of the Act deals with above policies of assurance. Section 11 of the Married Women's Property Act 1882 (c.75) (money paid under policy of insurance not to form part of the estate of the insured) applies in relation to a policy of assurance:

a) effected by a civil partner on his own life, and
b) expressed to be for the benefit of his civil partner, or of his children, or of his civil partner and children, or any of them, as it applies in relation to a policy of assurance effected by a husband and expressed to be for the benefit of his wife, or of his children, or of his wife and children, or of any of them.

Wills, administration of estates and family provision

Section 71 deals with wills and estates administration and states that schedule 4 to the Act amends enactments relating to wills, administration of estates and family provisions so that they apply in civil partnerships as they apply to marriages.

Financial relief for civil partners and children of the family

Section 72 of the Act deals with financial relief during a proceedings to end a civil partnership. Subsection (1) of section 72 states that Schedule 5 to the Act makes provision for financial relief in connection with civil partnerships that corresponds to provision made for financial relief in connection with marriages by part 2 of the Matrimonial Causes Act 1973 (c.18).

Subsection (2) states that any rule of law under which any provision of Part 2 of the 1973 Act is interpreted as applying to dissolution of a marriage on the ground of presumed death is to be treated as applying (with any necessary modifications) in relation to the corresponding provision of Schedule 5.

Subsection (3) states that Schedule 6 to the Act makes provision for financial relief in connection with civil partnerships that corresponds to provision made for financial relief in connection with marriages by the Domestic Proceedings and Magistrates Court Act 1978 (c.22).

Subsection (4) Schedule 7 to the Act makes provision for financial relief in England and Wales after a civil partnership has been dissolved or annulled, or civil partners have been legally separated, in a country outside the British Islands.

****

Chapter 6.

Civil Partnership Agreements

Civil partnership agreements unenforceable

Section 73 of the Civil Partnerships Act deals with civil partnership agreements and their contractual and other nature.

Subsection (1) of section 73 states that a civil partnership agreement does not under the law of England and Wales have effect as a contract giving rise to legal rights.

Subsection (2) states that no action lies in England and Wales for breach of a civil partnership agreement, whatever the law applicable to the agreement.

Subsection (2) states that in this section and section 74 (below) 'civil partnership agreement' means an agreement between two people:

a)   to register as civil partners of each other-

(i)   in England and Wales (under this part),
(ii)   in Scotland (in Part 3),
(iii)   in Northern Ireland (under Part 4), or
(iv)   outside the United Kingdom under an order in Council made under chapter 1 of Part 5 (registration at British Consulates etc, or by armed forces personnel) or

b)   to enter into an overseas relationship.

Subsection (4) states that this section applies in relation to civil partnership agreements whether entered into before or after this section comes into force, but does not affect any action commenced before it comes into force.

Property where civil partnership agreement is terminated

Subsection (1) of section 74 states that section 74 applies if a civil partnership agreement is terminated. Subsection (2) states that section 65 (contributions by civil partners to property improvements) applies, in relation to any property in which either or both of the parties to the agreement had a beneficial interest while the agreement was in force, as it applies in relation to property in which a civil partner has a beneficial interest.

Subsection (3) states that sections 66 and 67 (disputes between civil partners about property) apply to any dispute between or claim by one of the parties in relation to property in which either or both had a beneficial interest while the agreement was in force, as if the parties were civil partners of each other.

Subsection (4) states that an application made under section 66 or 67 by virtue of subsection (3) must be made within 3 years of the termination of the agreement.

Subsection (5) states that a party to a civil partnership agreement who makes a gift of property to the other party on the condition (express or implied) that it is to be returned if the agreement is terminated is not prevented from recovering the property merely because of his having terminated the agreement.

Chapter 7.

Civil Partnerships and Children

Children

Parental responsibility, children of the family and relatives

The welfare of children generally is of the utmost importance and Section 75 of the Civil Partnerships Act 2004 deals with the responsibility of civil partners to children and family following a civil partnership.

Subsection (1) of section 75 states that the Children's Act 1989 (c.41) (the 1989 Act) is amended as follows.

Subsection (2) defines the amendment, in section 4A(1)(acquisition of parental responsibility by stepparent after 'is married to' insert 'or a civil partner of'.

Subsection (3) states in section 105(1) (interpretation) for the definition of 'child of the family' (in relation to the parties to a marriage) substitute-

"child of the family", in relation to parties to a marriage, or two people who are civil partners of each other, means-

a) a child of both of them, and
b) any other child, other than a child placed with them as foster parents by a local authority or voluntary organisation, who has been treated by both of them as a child of their family".

Subsection (4) states that in the definition of "relative" in section 105(1), for "by affinity" substitute "by marriage or civil partnership".

Guardianship

Section 76 of the Act deals with guardianship of children. In section 6 of the 1989 Act (guardians: revocation and disclaimer) after subsection 3(A) insert-

"(3B) An appointment under section 5(3) or (4) (including one made in an unrevoked will or codicil) is revoked if the person appointed is the civil partner of the person who made the appointment and either-

a) an order of the court of civil jurisdiction in England and Wales dissolves or annuls the civil partnership, or
b) the civil partnership is dissolved or annulled and the dissolution or annulment is entitled to recognition in England and Wales by virtue of Chapter 3 of Part 5 of the Civil partnership Act 2004, unless a contrary intention appears by appointment.

Entitlement to apply for residence or contact order

Section 77 of the Act deals with entitlement to apply for residence or contact order. In section 10(5) of the 1989 Act (persons entitled to apply for residence or contact order) after paragraph (a) insert-

" (as) any civil partner in a civil partnership (whether or not subsisting) in relation to whom the child is a child of the family".

Financial provision for children

Section 78 of the Act deals with financial provision for children. Subsection (1) of section 78 amends Schedule 1 to the 1989 Act (financial provision for children) as follows in subsection (2).

In paragraph 2(6) (meaning of periodical payments order) after paragraph (d) insert-
" (e) Part 1 or 9 of Schedule 5 to the Civil partnership Act 2004 (financial relief in the High Court or a county court etc);

(f) Schedule 6 to the 2004 Act (financial relief in the magistrate's court etc),".

Subsection (3) states that in paragraph 15(2) (person with whom a child lives or is to live) after "husband or wife" insert "or civil partner".

Subsection (4) states for paragraph 16(2) (extended meaning of "parent") substitute-

"(2) In this Schedule, except paragraphs 2 and 15, "parent" includes-

a) any party to a marriage (whether or not subsisting) in relation to whom the child concerned is a child of the family, and
b) any civil partner in a civil partnership (whether or not subsisting) in relation to whom the child concerned is a child of the family;

and for this purpose any reference to either parent or both parents shall be read as a reference to any parent of his and to all of his parents".

Adoption

Section 79 of the Act deals with civil partnership and adoption. Subsection (1) amends the Adoption and Children Act of 2002 (c.38) as follow.

Subsection (2) states in section 21 (placement orders) in subsection (4)(c) after "child marries" insert "forms a civil partnership".

Subsection (3) states in section 47 (condition for making adoption orders) after subsection (8) insert-

"(8A) An adoption order may not be made in relation to a person who is or has been a civil partner".

Subsection (4) states in section 51 (adoption by one person), in subsection (1) after " is not married" insert "or a civil partner".
Subsection (5) states after section 51(3) insert-

"(3A) An adoption order may be made on the application of one person who has attained the age of 21 years and is a civil partner if the court is satisfied that-

  a) the persons civil partner cannot be found
  b) the civil partners have separated and are living apart, and the separation is likely to be permanent, or
  c) the persons civil partner is by reason of ill health, whether physical or mental, incapable of making an application for an adoption order".

Subsection (6) states in section 64 (other provisions to be made by regulations) in subsection (5) for "or marriage" substitute "marriage or civil partnership".

Subsection (7) states in section 74(1) (enactments for whose purposes section 67 does not apply) for paragraph (a) substitute-

"(a) section 1 of and Schedule 1 to the Marriage Act 1949 or Schedule 1 to the Civil Partnership Act 2004 (prohibited degrees of kindred and affinity).

Subsection (8) states in section 79 (connections between the register and birth records) , in subsection (7)-

  a) in paragraph (b) after "intends to be married" insert "or forms a civil partnership" and
  b) for "the person whom the applicant intends to marry" substitute "the intended spouse or civil partner".

Subsection (9) states in section 81 (Adoption Contact Register: supplementary), in subsection (2) for "or marriage" substitute marriage or civil partnership".

Subsection (10) states in section 98 (pre-commencement adoptions: information), in subsection (7), in the definition of "relative" for "or marriage" substitute "marriage or civil partnership".

Subsection (11) states in section 144 (interpretation), in the definition of "relative" in subsection (1), after "by marriage" insert "or civil partnership".

Subsection (12) states in section 144(4) (meaning of "couple"), after paragraph (a) insert-

"(aa) two people who are civil partners of each other, or"

Chapter 8.

Miscellaneous Provisions

Miscellaneous

False statements with reference to civil partnerships

Section 80 of the Civil Partnerships Act 2004 deals with the making of false statements when entering into a civil partnership.

Subsection 1 states that a person commits an offence if:

a) for the purpose of procuring the formation of a civil partnership, or a document mentioned in subsection (2) below, he-

    (i)   makes or signs a declaration required under this Part or Part 5, or

    (ii)   gives a notice so required.

knowing that the declaration, notice or certificate is false,

b) for the purpose of a record being made in any register relating to civil partnerships, he-

    (i)   makes a statement as to any information which is required to be registered under this Part or Part 5, or

    (ii)   causes such a statement to be made,

knowing that this statement is false.

(c) he forbids the issue of a document mentioned in subsection (2)(a) or (b) by representing himself to be a person whose consent to a civil partnership between a child and another person is required under this Part or Part 5, knowing the representation to be false, or

(d) with respect to a declaration made under paragraph 5(1) of Schedule 1 he makes a statement mentioned in paragraph 6 of that Schedule which he knows to be false in a material particular.

Subsection (2) states that the documents are:

a) a civil partnership schedule or a Registrar General's licence under chapter 1;
b) a document required by an order in council under section 210 or 211 as an authority for two people to register as civil partners of each other,
c) a certificate of no impediment under s240.

Subsection (3) states a person guilty of an offence under subsection (1) is liable-

a) on conviction on indictment, to imprisonment for a term not exceeding 7 years or to a fine or both,
b) on summary conviction, to a fine not exceeding the statutory maximum.

Subsection (4) states that the Perjury Act 1911 (c.6) has effect as if this section were contained within it.

Housing and Tenancies

Section 81 deals with housing and tenancies. Schedule 8 to the Act (see appendix) amends certain enactments relating to housing and tenancies.

Family homes and Domestic violence

Section 82 deals with family homes and domestic violence. Schedule 9 (see appendix) amends Part 4 of the Family Law Act 1996 (c.27) and related enactments so that they apply in relation to civil partnerships as they apply in relation to marriages.

Fatal accident claims

Section 83 deals with fatal accident claims. Subsection (1) of section 83 amends the Fatal Accidents Act 1976 (c.30) as follows. Subsection (2) provides the amendment. In section 1(3) (meaning of "dependant" for purposes of right of action for wrongful action causing death) after paragraph (a) insert-

"(aa) the civil partner or former civil partner of the deceased".

Subsection (3) states in paragraph (b)(iii) of section 1(3) after "wife" insert "or civil partner".

Subsection (4) states after paragraph (f) of section 1(3) insert-

"(fa) any person (not being a child of the deceased) who, in the case of any civil partnership in which the deceased was at any time a civil partner, was treated by the deceased as a child of the family in relation to that civil partnership".

Subsection (5) states after section 1(4) insert-

"(4A) The reference to the former civil partner of the deceased in subsection (3)(aa) above includes a reference to a person whose civil partnership with the deceased has been annulled as well as a person whose civil partnership with the deceased has been dissolved".

Subsection 6 states in section 1(5)(a), for "by affinity" substitute "by marriage or civil partnership".

Subsection (7) states in section 1A(2) (persons for whose benefit claim for bereavement damages may be made)-

a) in paragraph (a) after "wife or husband" insert "or civil partner" and

b) in paragraph (b), after "was never married" insert "or a civil partner".

Evidence

Section 84 deals with the giving of evidence. Subsection (1) of section 84 states that any enactment or rule of law relating to the giving of evidence by a spouse applies in relation to a civil partner as it applies in relation to a spouse. Subsection (2) states that subsection (1) is subject to any specific amendment made by or under this Act which relates to the giving of evidence by a civil partner.

Subsection (3) states that for the avoidance of doubt, in any such amendment reference to a persons civil partner do not include a former civil partner.

Subsection (4) states that references to subsections (1) and (2) to giving evidence are to giving evidence in any way (whether by supplying information, making discovery, producing documents or otherwise.)

Subsection (5) states that any rule of law:

a) which is preserved by section 7(3) of the Civil Evidence Act 1995 (c.38) or section 118(1) of the Criminal Justice Act 2003 (c.44) and

b) under which in any proceedings evidence of reputation or family tradition is admissible for the purpose of proving or disproving the existence of a marriage,

is to be treated as applying in an equivalent way for the purpose of proving or disproving the existence of a civil partnership.

Chapter 9.

Part 5. Civil Partnerships Formed or Dissolved Abroad

Registration outside U.K. under Order in Council.

Registration at British Consulates etc.
Section 210 of the CPA 2004 deals with registration at British Consulates and other matters.

Subsection (1) of section 210 states that Her Majesty may by Order in Council make provision for two people to register as civil partners of each other:

a) in prescribed countries or territories outside the United Kingdom, and

b) in the presence of a prescribed officer of Her Majesty's Diplomatic Service

in cases where the officer is satisfied that the conditions in subsection (2) below are met.

Subsection (2) lays out those conditions as follows:

a) at least one of the proposed civil partners is a United Kingdom national,

b) the proposed civil partners would have been eligible to register as civil partners of each other in such part of the United Kingdom as is determined in accordance with the order,

c) the authorities of the countries or territory in which it is proposed that they register as civil partners will not object to the registration, and

d) insufficient facilities exist for them to enter into an overseas relationship under the law of that country or territory.

Subsection (3) states that an officer is not required to allow two people to register as civil partners of each other if in his opinion the formation of a civil partnership between them would be inconsistent with international law or the comity of nations.

Subsection (4) states that an Order in Council under this section may make provision for appeals against a refusal, in reliance on subsection (3), to allow two people to register as civil partners of each other.

Subsection (5) states that an Order in Council under this section may provide that two people who register as civil partners of each other under such an order are to be treated for the purposes of sections 221(1)(c)(i) and(2)(c)(i),222©,224(b),225(c)(i) and (3)(c)(i),229(c)(i) and (2)(c)(i),230(c) and 232(b)(i) of the Presumption of Death (Scotland) Act 1977 (c.27) as if they had done so in the part of the United Kingdom determined as mentioned in subsection (2)(b).

Registration by armed forces personnel

Section 211 of the Act deals with armed forces personnel. Subsection (1) of section 211 states that her majesty may by Order in Council make provision for two people to register as civil partners of each other:

a) in prescribed countries or territories outside the United Kingdom, and

b) in the presence of an officer appointed by virtue of the Registration of Births, Deaths and marriages (Special Provisions) Act 1957 (c.58).

in cases where the officer is satisfied that the conditions in subsection (2) below are met. Subsection (2) lays out those conditions:

a)   at least one of the proposed civil partners-

(i)   is a member of a part of Her Majesty's forces serving in the country or territory,

(ii)   is employed in the country or territory in such other capacity as may be prescribed, or

(iii)   is a child of a person falling within sub-paragraph (i) or (ii) and has his home with that person in that country or territory,

(b) the proposed civil partners would have been eligible to register as civil partners of each other in such part of the United Kingdom as is determined in accordance with the Order, and

(c) such other requirements as may be prescribed are complied with.

Subsection (3) states that in determining for the purposes of sub-section (2) whether one person is the child of another, a person who is or was treated by another as a child of the family in relation to:

a)   a marriage to which the other is or was a party, or
b)   a civil partnership in which the other is or was a civil partner

is to be regarded as the other's child.

Subsection (4) states that an Order in Council under this section may provide that two people who register as civil partners of each other under such an order are to be treated for the purposes of section 221(1)(c)(i) and (2)(c)(i),222 (c), 224(b) 225(1) (c) (i) 229(1)(c) (i) and (2) (c) (i) 230 (c) and 232 (b) and section 1 (3)(c)(i) of the Presumption of Death (Scotland) Act 1977 (c.27) as if they had done so in the part of the United Kingdom determined in accordance with subsection (2)(b).

Subsection 5 states that any references made in this section:

a) to a country or territory outside the United Kingdom,
b) to forces serving in such a country or territory, and
c) to persons employed in such a country or territory,

include references to ships which are for the time being in the waters of a country or territory outside the United Kingdom, to forces serving in any such ship and to persons employed in any such ship.

****

Chapter 10.

Overseas Relationships Treated as Civil Partnerships

Meaning of overseas relationship

Section 212 of the Act deals further with overseas relationships. Subsection (1) states that for the purposes of this Act an overseas relationship is a relationship which:

a) is either a specified relationship or a relationship which meets the general conditions, and

b) is registered (whether before or after the passing of this Act) with a responsible authority in a country or territory outside the United Kingdom, by two people-

   (i) who under the relevant law are of the same sex at the time when they do so, and

   (ii) neither of whom is already a civil partner or lawfully married.

Subsection (2) states that in this chapter, "the relevant law" means the law of the country or territory where the relationship is registered (including its rules of private international law).

Specified relationships

Section 213 subsection (1) deals with specified relationships, as defined by Schedule 20 to the Act. Subsection (2) states that the Secretary of State may by an order amend Schedule 20 by:

a) adding a relationship,

b) amending the description of a relationship, and

c) omitting a relationship.

Subsection (3) states that no order may be made under this section without the consent of the Scottish Ministers and the Department of Finance and Personnel.

Subsection (4) states that the power to make an order under this section is excercisable by statutory instrument.

Subsection (5) states that an order which contains any provision (whether alone or with other provisions) amending Schedule 20 by-

a) amending the description of a relationship, or
b) omitting a relationship,

may not be made unless a draft of the statutory instrument containing the order is laid before, and approved by a resolution of, each house of parliament.

The general conditions
Section 214 deals with general conditions and civil partnerships abroad. The general conditions are that, under the relevant law:
a) the relationship may not be entered into if either of the parties is already a party to a relationship of that kind or lawfully married,
b) the relationship is of an indeterminate duration, and
c) the effect of entering into it is that the parties are-

    (i)   treated as a couple either generally or for specified purposes, or
    (ii)   treated as married.

Overseas relationships treated as civil partnerships: the general rule
Section 215 deals with overseas relationships which are treated as civil partnerships. Subsection (10 states that two people are to be treated as

having formed a civil partnership as a result of having registered an overseas relationship if, under the relevant law, they:

a) had capacity to enter into the relationship, and
b) met all requirements necessary to ensure the formal validity of the relationship.

Subsection (2) states that subject to subsection (3) below, the time when they are to be treated as having formed the civil partnership is the time when the overseas relationship is registered (under the relevant law) as having been entered into.

Subsection (3) states that if the overseas relationship is registered (under the relevant law) as having been entered into before this section comes into force, the time when they are treated as having formed a civil partnership is the time when this section comes into force.

Subsection (4) states that if:

a) before this section comes into force, a dissolution or annulment of the overseas relationship was obtained outside the United Kingdom, and
b) the dissolution or annulment would be recognised under Chapter 3 if the overseas relationship had been treated as a civil partnership at the time of the dissolution or annulment,

subsection (3) does not apply and subsections (1) and (2) have effect subject to subsection (5).

Subsection (5) states that the overseas relationship is not to be treated as having been a civil partnership for the purposes of any provisions except:

a) Schedules 7, 11 and 17 (financial relief in United Kingdom after dissolution or annulment obtained outside the United Kingdom);
b) Such provisions as are specified (with or without modifications) in an order under s 259;
c) Chapter 3 (so far as necessary for the purposes of paragraphs (a) and (b)).

Subsection (6) that this section is subject to sections 216, 217 and 218.

The same sex requirement

Section 216 deals with the same sex requirement. Subsection (1) states that two people are not to be treated as having formed a civil partnership as a result of having registered an overseas relationship if, at the critical time, they were not of the same sex under United Kingdom law.

Subsection (2) states that if a full gender recognition certificate is issued under the 2004 Act to a person who has registered an overseas relationship which is within subsection (4) below after the issue of the certificate the relationship is no longer prevented from being treated as a civil partnership on the ground that, at the critical time, the parties were not of the same sex.

Subsection (3) states that, however, subsection (2) does not apply to an overseas relationship which is within subsection (4) below if either of the parties has formed a subsequent civil partnership or lawful marriage.

Subsection (4) states that an overseas relationship is within this section if (and only if) at the time mentioned in section 215(2)-

a) one of the parties ("A") was regarded under the relevant law as having changed gender (but was not regarded under United Kingdom law as having done so), and

b) the other party was (under United Kingdom law) of the gender to which A had changed under the relevant law.

Subsection (5) states that, in this section-

"the critical time" means the time determined in accordance with section 215(2) or (as the case may be) (3);

"the 2004 Act" means the Gender Recognition Act 2004 (c.7); "United Kingdom law" means any enactment or rule of law applying in England and Wales, Scotland and Northern Ireland.

Subsection (6) states that nothing in this section prevents the exercise of any enforceable community right.

Persons domiciled in a part of the United Kingdom
Section 217 deals with domicile in a part of the United Kingdom. Subsection 1 (2) of section 217 applies if an overseas relationship has been registered by a person who was at the time mentioned in section 215 (2) domiciled in England and Wales.

Subsection (2) states that the two people concerned are not to be treated as having formed a civil partnership if, at the time mentioned in section 215 (2)-

a) either of them was under 16, or
b) they would have been within prohibited degrees of relationship under Part 1 of schedule 1 if they had been registering as civil partners of each other in England and Wales.

Subsection (3) states that subsection (4) applies if an overseas relationship has been registered by a person who at the time mentioned in section 215 (2) was domiciled in Scotland.

Subsection (4) states that the two people concerned are not to be treated as having formed a civil partnership if, at the time mentioned in section 215 (2), they were not eligible by virtue of paragraph (b), (c) or (e) of section 86(1) to register in Scotland as civil partners of each other.

Subsection (5) states that subsection (6) applies if an overseas relationship has been registered by a person who at the time mentioned in section 215(2) was domiciled in Northern Ireland.

Subsection (6) states that the two people concerned are not to be treated as having formed a civil partnership if, at the time mentioned in s125 (2)-

a) either of them was under 16,or
b) b) they would have been within prohibited degrees of relationship under Schedule 12 if they had been registering as civil partners of each other in Northern Ireland.

The public policy exception

Section 218 states that two people are not to be treated as having formed a civil partnership as a result of having entered into an overseas relationship if it would be manifestly contrary to public policy to recognise the capacity under the relevant law, of one or both of them to enter into the relationship.

****

Chapter 11.

Marriage (Same Sex Couples) Act 2013

Following on from the introduction of the Civil Partnerships Act 2004, the introduction of the Marriage (Same Sex Couples) Act 2013 has introduced the right of marriage and religious ceremony for same sex couples. As might be imagined, this didn't become law without a fight. Nevertheless, it is now law and the following chapters outline the Act and the rights it confers on same sex couples.

The main provisions of the Marriage (Same Sex Couples) Act 2013 are:

1. To allow same sex couples to marry in a civil ceremony;
2. To allow same sex couples to marry in a religious ceremony where the religious organisation has "opted in"
3. To enable civil partners to convert their civil partnership into a marriage;
4. To enable married individuals to change their legal gender without having to end their marriage.

Marriage of same sex couples

Those couples not in an existing legal relationship will be able to give notice of marriage from **Thursday 13th March 2014**. The first marriage for same sex couples will therefore be able to take place on Saturday 29th March 2014. This does not apply to a couple who are currently in a civil partnership. The arrangements for allowing the conversion of civil partnerships into marriages, and allowing people who change their legal gender to remain in their marriage, will follow later.

Background

Under the previous law, a marriage could only be between a man and a woman. Marriage law in England and Wales is based on where the marriage ceremony takes place. The Marriage Act 1949 (the "Marriage Act") sets out that a marriage can be solemnized (solemnization is the legal ceremony which gives effect to the marriage) either in religious buildings, through a religious ceremony, or on secular (non-religious) premises, through a civil ceremony. The law makes particular provision relating to marriage according to the rites and ceremonies of the Church of England and the Church in Wales, and to marriages according to the rites and usages of the Jewish religion and the Quakers (Society of Friends).

As we have seen in the previous chapters, same sex couples may register a civil partnership under the Civil Partnership Act 2004 (the "Civil Partnership Act"). A civil partnership is only available to same sex couples and can only be conducted through a civil ceremony, although following legislative change in 2011 this may be held in a religious building.

Church of England

The position of the Church of England is different from that of other religious organisations for three main reasons:

- as the established Church, its Canons (church laws) form part of the law of the land;
- as the established Church, it can amend or repeal primary legislation through a Measure passed by its Synod, provided the Measure is subsequently approved by both Houses of Parliament and receives Royal Assent;
- its clergy are under a common law duty to marry a parishioner in his or her parish church. The Church in Wales has a similar duty by virtue of it previously being established (it became disestablished in 1920).

Summary of the Act

The main purpose of the Act is to enable same sex couples to marry, either in a civil ceremony (i.e. a civil ceremony in a register office or approved premises e.g. a hotel) or, provided that the religious organisation concerned is in agreement, on religious premises, with the marriage being solemnized through a religious ceremony.

Key elements of the Act:

- provide that same sex couples can get married in England and Wales;

- provide that such marriages are the same as marriages between a man and a woman under the law of England and Wales;

- permit marriage of same sex couples by way of a civil ceremony;

- permit marriage of same sex couples according to religious rites and usages where a religious organisation has opted in to that process (with the exception of the Church of England and the Church in Wales);

- provide a process by which the Church in Wales can request and obtain legislative change to allow marriages of same sex couples according to its rites if it wishes to do so;

- provide that there will be no obligation or compulsion on religious organisations or individuals to carry out or participate in a religious marriage ceremony of a same sex couple;

- provide protection under equality law for religious organisations and individuals who do not wish to marry same sex couples in a religious ceremony;

provide for reviews of:

- whether an order should be made permitting belief organisations to solemnize marriages and to consider what provision should be made in the order;

- the operation and future of the Civil Partnership Act in England and Wales;

- survivor benefits under occupational pension schemes.

The Act does not remove the availability of civil partnerships for same sex couples. There is provision in the Act for those in a civil partnership to convert that relationship to a marriage if they choose to do so.

Religious organisations and their representatives who do not wish to marry same sex couples are protected from being compelled to do so through a series of religious protections, including:

- an explicit provision in the Act that no religious organisation can be compelled to opt in to marry same sex couples or to permit this to happen in their place of worship, and no religious organisation or individual can be compelled to conduct religious same sex marriage ceremonies;

- amendments which the Act makes to the Equality Act 2010, to provide that it is not unlawful discrimination for a religious organisation or individual to refuse to marry a same sex couple in a religious ceremony;

- an "opt-in" mechanism whereby a marriage of a same sex couple cannot be carried out on religious premises or with a religious ceremony without the express consent of the religious organisation's governing body;

- ensuring that the Act does not interfere with Anglican Canon law or ecclesiastical law;

- ensuring that the common law duty on Church of England and Church in Wales clergy to marry parishioners does not extend to same sex couples.

The Act does not amend marriage legislation to allow Church of England clergy to solemnize marriage of same sex couples according to its rites, and specific provision is made to ensure that the nature of marriage in Anglican Canon law is unaltered. Specific provision is made to ensure that the common law duty to marry parishioners, which applies to the clergy of both the Church of England and the Church in Wales, (and any corresponding right of parishioners to be married by such clergy) does not extend to same sex couples. In order to be able to solemnize marriages of same sex couples, therefore, the Church of England would have to put a Measure before Parliament amending the law to allow this to happen. The Church in Wales is unable to do this, and so the Act provides a power by which this must be done by the Lord Chancellor, by order, should the Governing Body of the Church in Wales request it.

The Act also contains a number of other related provisions, including provisions that will enable a person to change their legal gender without ending their existing marriage; provisions dealing with consular marriage and marriage on armed forces bases overseas; and recognition of certain marriages of same sex couples formed outside England and Wales. There are also consequential and interpretative provisions clarifying how the new law will affect a number of matters, such as state and occupational pensions.

A number of the provisions of the Act are to be given effect through subordinate legislation. Further details of these delegated powers are included in the Delegated Powers Memorandum and explained in the commentary on sections and schedules below.

Overview of the structure of the Act

The Act is largely an amending Act, making amendments to various pieces of primary legislation including:

the Marriage Act 1949,

the Equality Act 2010,

the Marriage (Registrar General's Licence) Act 1970,

the Matrimonial Causes Act 1973,

the Domicile and Matrimonial Proceedings Act 1973,

the Social Security Contributions and Benefits Act 1992,

the Pension Schemes Act 1993,

the Civil Partnership Act 2004,

the Gender Recognition Act 2004.

The Act consists of 21 sections and 7 schedules arranged as follows:

Part 1 (sections 1-11) (Marriage of same sex couples in England and Wales) contains the main provisions of the Act relating to marriage of same sex couples and Schedules 1 to 4 contain consequential and interpretative provisions relating to Part 1.

Part 2 (sections 12-16) (Other provisions relating to marriage and civil partnership) deal with the change of legal gender of a married person or civil partner and marriage overseas (as do Schedules 5 and 6) and with the reviews of marriage by belief organisations, of the operation and future of the Civil Partnership Act in England and Wales and of survivor benefits under occupational pension schemes.

Part 3 (sections 17-21) (Final provisions) and Schedule 7 contain the standard technical provisions of the Act, including order-making powers and procedures, interpretation, extent and commencement.

Territorial extent and application

General

The territorial extent and application of the Act is England and Wales only, except for particular provisions as follows:

Provisions which extend to Scotland

In Part 1 of the Act, section 10(3), which gives effect to Schedule 2. Schedule 2 deals with the treatment in the rest of the United Kingdom of marriages of same sex couples under the law of England and Wales.

Part 2 (other than sections 14 and 15).

All of Part 3.

Provisions which extend to Northern Ireland

In Part 1 of the Act, section 10(3) and Schedule 2.

Part 2 (other than the repeal of the Foreign Marriage Act 1892 made by section 13(2), sections 14 to 16, Part 2 of Schedule 5 and paragraphs 4, 5, 10 and 11 of Schedule 6).

All of Part 3.

Scotland

17.The Act provides for marriage of same sex couples to be lawful in England and Wales only. Marriage is an area which is a devolved matter for Scotland, meaning that it is something which is within the legislative powers of the Scottish Parliament. The Act would have certain effects in Scotland, however. It allows for the consequential amendment to legislation in Scotland, as a result of marriage for same sex couples coming into force in England and Wales. If this happens before such time as marriage of same sex couples is lawful in Scotland, the Act contains a power to secure that a marriage of a same sex couple entered into in England and Wales is treated as a civil partnership in Scotland. The provision which the Act makes about consular marriage and marriage on armed forces bases overseas also involves amendment of the law in Scotland. There are also amendments to the law in Scotland as it relates to re-issuing and correcting errors in gender recognition certificates and fraud proceedings under the Gender Recognition Act 2004. Consequential provision of the law in Scotland may also be made as a result of those changes. The statutory review of survivor benefits under occupational pension schemes will extend to Scotland, as well as to England and Wales, and any subsequent order may amend Scottish legislation.

This Act contains provisions that triggered the Sewel Convention. The provisions relate to the power for the Secretary of State to make an order for a marriage of a same sex couple solemnized in England and Wales to be treated as a civil partnership under the law of Scotland; the power for the Secretary of State to make consequential amendments to the law of Scotland in devolved areas; the power for the Queen to make Orders in Council about how UK consulates overseas carry out marriages and how marriage can take place on armed forces bases overseas insofar as this affects the law of Scotland. The Sewel Convention provides that Westminster will not normally legislate with regard to devolved matters in Scotland without the consent of the Scottish Parliament. The Scottish Parliament agreed a Legislative Consent Motion in these terms on 11 June 2013. In making any order or regulations under the Act which contain provision that would otherwise be within the legislative competence of the Scottish Parliament, the Secretary of State or Lord Chancellor will first have to obtain the consent of the Scottish Ministers.

Wales

The Act allows for marriage of same sex couples in Wales, where the effect will be the same as that in England. Marriage of same sex couples will be equivalent to marriage of opposite sex couples except in certain cases. Existing legislation will be understood as applying to same sex couples as it has done until now to opposite sex couples. New legislation will be read as applying in the same way to same sex couples as to opposite sex couples.

As explained above, the Act does not permit religious marriage ceremonies in accordance with the rites of the Church in Wales. However, it does contain provision for the Church in Wales to request a change in the law to enable the marriage of same sex couples according to the rites of the Church in Wales, should it wish to do so (see section 8 of the Act).

Northern Ireland

Marriage is an area which is a devolved matter for Northern Ireland. The Act does not affect Northern Ireland directly, except as follows:

- there are amendments to the law in Northern Ireland as it relates to re-issuing and correcting errors in gender recognition certificates and fraud proceedings under the Gender Recognition Act 2004;

- the Act provides that marriages of same sex couples under the law of England and Wales will be treated as civil partnerships under the law of Northern Ireland.

The UK Government has proceeded in accordance with the convention that the UK Parliament does not normally legislate with regard to devolved matters in Northern Ireland except with the agreement of the Northern Ireland legislature. There are a number of provisions within the Act which triggered the convention. In addition to the provision of the Act which affects Northern Ireland directly (the treatment of same sex couples married in England and Wales), another provision which triggered that convention is a power for the Secretary of State to make consequential amendments in devolved areas. Other similar provisions include those which relate to the change of legal gender of married persons or civil partners. Any orders or regulations made under the Act which make provision that would otherwise be within the legislative competence of the Northern Ireland Assembly will require the consent of the Department of Finance and Personnel. Section 13 of the Act repeals the Foreign Marriage Act 1892, and Schedule 6 provides for a new regime of consular marriages and marriages on armed forces bases overseas in respect of both opposite sex and same sex couples. The Northern Ireland Assembly made a decision not to include section 13 of, or Schedule 6 to, the Act in the Legislative Consent Motion it passed on 24 June 2013. As a result, the Act excludes Northern Ireland from the new provisions regarding consular marriage and marriage on armed forces bases overseas.

****

Chapter 12.

Sections and Schedules to the Act

Parts 1-3

Part 1 – Marriage of same sex couples in England and Wales
Extension of marriage

Section 1 – Extension of marriage to same sex couples

Section 1 makes marriage of same sex couples lawful in England and Wales and sets out the legislative provisions under which same sex couples may marry. It ensures there is no obligation on the clergy of the Church of England and the Church in Wales to marry same sex couples and makes particular provision to avoid conflict with the Canons of the Church of England.

Under subsection (2) marriages of same sex couples may be solemnized in accordance with:

Part 3 of the Marriage Act, which provides for civil marriage ceremonies in register offices or approved premises such as hotels; and, if the relevant religious organisation has opted in to marry same sex couples, marriages in religious buildings (other than those of the Church of England or Church in Wales), or according to the usages of the Jewish religion or Quakers (Society of Friends) and for certain marriages for detained or house-bound persons;

Part 5 of the Marriage Act, which provides for marriages in naval, military and air force chapels (but not according to the rites of the Church of England or Church in Wales);

- the Marriage (Registrar General's Licence) Act 1970, which provides for "deathbed" marriages outside registered premises; or

- an Order in Council made under Part 1 or 3 of Schedule 6 to the Act, which may provide for marriages overseas in the presence of a consular officer or for marriage overseas on armed forces bases.

The effect of subsection (3) is to preserve the integrity of the Canon law of the Church of England in relation to marriage. Under the Submission of the Clergy Act 1533, Canon law cannot be contrary to general law. In particular, Canon B30 (paragraph 1) states that "The Church of England affirms, according to our Lord's teaching, that marriage is in its nature a union permanent and lifelong, for better for worse, till death them do part, of one man with one woman…".

Subsection (3) therefore provides that the maintenance of Canon B30 in particular by the Church of England is not contrary to the general law which enables same sex couples to marry.

Subsections (4) and (5) provide that any duty of a member of the clergy of the Church of England or the Church in Wales to solemnize a marriage does not extend to same sex couples. In addition, any corresponding right of parishioners to be married by such clergy does not extend to same sex couples. The effect of this is that the common law duty on the clergy of the Church of England and the Church in Wales to marry parishioners is not extended to same sex couples.

Religious protection
Section 2 – Marriage according to religious rites: no compulsion to solemnize etc

Section 2 protects individuals and religious organisations who do not wish to conduct or participate in a religious marriage ceremony on the ground that it is a marriage of a same sex couple.

Subsection (1) states that individuals and religious organisations may not be compelled by any means to carry out an "opt-in activity", which is defined in subsection (3) to mean the various types of activity relating to the decision of a religious organisation to opt in to solemnizing marriages of same sex couples. Subsection (1) also states that they cannot be compelled to refrain from carrying out an "opt-out activity", defined to mean an activity which reverses or modifies the effect of an opt-in activity.

Subsection (2) makes clear that individuals may not be compelled by any means to carry out, attend or take part in a religious marriage ceremony of a same sex couple. It also makes clear that individuals and religious organisations may not be compelled to consent to religious marriage ceremonies of same sex couples being conducted. In each case this must be where the individuals or religious organisations do not wish to carry out the specified conduct because it concerns the marriage of a same sex couple.

The concept of "compulsion" is a broad one, which would include, but not be limited to, attempts to use criminal or civil law, contractual clauses, or the imposition of any detriment to force a person to carry out such an activity. The section provides no specific remedy, but makes clear that no attempt at such compulsion will be upheld. The remedy for any action taken to compel someone would depend on the nature of the action taken.

Subsection (3) contains the definitions of "opt-in" activity and "opt-out activity", and subsection (4) defines various other terms used in the section. It also makes clear that the conduct of a marriage registrar, superintendent registrar or the Registrar General is not included in the protection provided by this section.

Subsection (5) inserts new subsections (5A) and (5B) into section 110 of the Equality Act 2010. Section 110(1) of the Equality Act 2010 makes an employee, or an agent for a principal, personally liable for unlawful acts they commit in the course of their employment, or under the authority of a principal, for which their employer or principal could also be held liable. New subsections (5A) and (5B) provide that an individual cannot be held personally liable under the Equality Act 2010 for a refusal to carry out the conduct specified in subsection (2) of this section where the reason is that the marriage is the marriage of a same sex couple.

Subsection (6) inserts a new Part 6A (Marriage of same sex couples in England and Wales) and paragraph 25A (Marriage according to religious rites: no compulsion to solemnize etc) into Schedule 3 to the Equality Act 2010. Schedule 3 deals with exceptions from the prohibition on discrimination in the provision of services and the exercise of public functions. New paragraph 25A provides that it is not unlawful discrimination under that Act for an individual or religious organisation not to carry out the conduct specified in subsection (2) where the reason is that the marriage is the marriage of a same sex couple.

Part 3 of the Marriage Act 1949
Section 3 – Marriage for which no opt-in necessary

Section 3 replaces the existing section 26 in Part 3 of the Marriage Act (Marriages which may be solemnized on the authority of superintendent registrar's certificate) with a new section 26 (Marriage of a man and a woman; marriage of same sex couples for which no opt-in necessary). The new section 26 replicates the existing section 26 for marriages between a man and a woman and further authorises certain marriages of same sex couples (by civil ceremony). New section 26 therefore authorises:

- religious marriage ceremonies between a man and a woman in registered buildings;

- civil marriage ceremonies for all couples in a register office;

- civil marriage ceremonies for all couples in approved premises (for example a hotel);

- religious marriage ceremonies between a man and a woman by the Quakers or those of the Jewish religion;

- marriages between a man and a woman one of whom is house-bound or detained;

- civil marriage ceremonies of a same sex couple, one of whom is house-bound or detained;

- marriages between a man and a woman in a church or chapel of the Church of England or the Church in Wales.

Therefore, civil marriage ceremonies of same sex couples are authorised under this section, but religious marriages of same sex couples are authorised under different provisions of the Marriage Act – these are inserted by sections 4 to 6 of this Act, which create arrangements for religious organisations other than the Church of England and Church in Wales to opt in to conducting marriages of same sex couples. Particular provision for the Church in Wales is contained in section 8.

This section will allow same sex couples to have a civil marriage ceremony on approved premises such as a hotel or stately home or in a register office, and will also allow the marriage by a registrar of a same sex couple where one of the couple is house-bound or detained at his or her usual place of residence. These marriage ceremonies do not require an opt-in. The remaining provisions of this section restate the provisions in relation to the marriage of opposite sex couples in both civil and religious ceremonies – these marriages also do not require an opt-in.

Section 4 – Opt-in: marriage in places of worship

Section 4 inserts a new section 26A (Opt-in to marriage of same sex couples: places of worship) into the Marriage Act. The effect of the section is to authorise religious marriage ceremonies of same sex couples in certified places of worship (where the relevant religious organisation has opted in and registered the place of worship to solemnize marriages of same sex couples).

New section 26A (subsection (1)) permits religious marriage ceremonies of same sex couples in a place of worship that has been specifically registered to solemnize marriages of same sex couples under section 43A ("an appropriately registered building"). New section 43A (inserted by paragraph 2 of Schedule 1 to the Act) sets out the procedure for the registration of a building for religious marriage ceremonies of same sex couples. Subsection (3) of section 26A provides that an application for registration under section 43A cannot be made without the written consent of the relevant governing authority of the religious organisation concerned. Subsection (4) of new section 26A defines what is meant by the "relevant governing authority". This definition leaves it open to religious organisations to define their governing authority as they wish for the purpose of giving consent to religious marriage of same sex couples.

Subsection (5) of new section 26A makes clear that the ability to opt in does not apply in respect of marriage according to the rites of the Church of England or the Church in Wales. In this Part of the Marriage Act, references to the Church of England include the Church in Wales.

Subsection (6) makes the provisions of section 26A subject to the provisions of sections 44A to 44C of the Marriage Act and any regulations made under any of these sections. Sections 44A to 44C are new sections inserted by paragraph 3 of Schedule 1 to the Act and make provision about registration of buildings for marriage of same sex couples where buildings are shared by more than one religious organisation.

Subsection (2) of section 4 brings into effect Schedule 1 (Registration of buildings etc). This will enable same sex couples to be married in religious ceremonies at certified places of worship where the religious organisation concerned has registered the building for the solemnization of marriages of same sex couples. There is no requirement for religious organisations to register their buildings and, if the organisation does not wish to solemnize marriages of same sex couples, it does not have to do so. This applies to all religious organisations except for the Church of England, the Church in Wales, the Society of Friends (Quakers) and those of the Jewish religion.

Section 5 – Opt-in: other religious ceremonies

Section 5 inserts a new section 26B into the Marriage Act. As mentioned above, three of the kinds of religious marriages of a man and a woman allowed by section 26 of the Marriage Act are marriages of Quakers; marriages according to the Jewish religion; and religious marriage ceremonies of people who are house-bound or detained, e.g. in prison. These marriages are not required to take place in a certified place of worship. New section 26B makes these kinds of marriage available to same sex couples, subject to the relevant opt-in procedure being followed.

The section provides that religious marriage ceremonies of same sex couples may take place without the need for registration of a building in the following circumstances:

- marriage in accordance with the religious practices of Quakers, as long as the recording clerk of the Society of

Friends in London has consented to marriages of same sex couples.

- marriage in a religious ceremony of the Jewish religion, as long as the relevant governing authority has consented to marriages of same sex couples. In this case the relevant governing authority will depend on the affiliation of the particular synagogue.

Where one or both of a same sex couple is house-bound or detained, they can marry through a religious ceremony of any religious organisation except the Church of England or Church in Wales, provided the relevant governing authority has given consent to marry same sex couples. In this case the relevant governing authority has the same definition as in section 26A of the Marriage Act. Marriages of Quakers and of people professing the Jewish religion cannot be authorised under this provision and must be authorised under the other provisions above.

Part 5 of the Marriage Act 1949
Section 6 – Armed forces chapels

Section 6 amends Part 5 of the Marriage Act, which deals with marriages in naval, military and air force chapels (referred to in these notes as military chapels). Under that Part, a marriage may take place in a military chapel which has been licensed under section 69 for the solemnization of marriages according to the rites of the Church of England or the Church in Wales, or registered under section 70 for the solemnization of marriages other than according to those rites. Section 6 amends Part 5 of the Marriage Act to make provision for the registration of military chapels for the solemnization of marriages of same sex couples through religious ceremonies, except in accordance with the rites of the Church of England or the Church in Wales.

Subsection (2) of section 6 amends section 68 of the Marriage Act so that provisions in Part 5 of that Act which apply to marriages of same sex couples do not apply to marriages according to the rites of the Church of England or the Church in Wales.

Subsection (3) of section 6 amends section 70 of the Marriage Act so as to provide that that section does not apply to marriages of same sex couples. However, subsection (4) inserts a new section 70A which allows registration of military chapels for marriages of same sex couples (otherwise than according to the rites of the Church of England or the Church in Wales). Where a chapel is registered under section 70A, section 70A(3) provides that section 70 applies (except the provision which excludes marriages of same sex couples) as if the chapel were registered under that section.

Under subsection (1) of the new section 70A a chapel may be registered by the Registrar General on the application of the Secretary of State. Under subsection (2) the procedural requirements of section 70 (for example, in relation to cancellation of registration, and publicising registration and cancellation) apply equally for the purposes of section 70A.

Subsections (5) and (6) of the new section 70A provide a power for the Secretary of State to make regulations about the registration of chapels under the section and the cancellation of registration, which may include provisions about the procedures to be followed and any consents that must be obtained before an application for registration may be made. Military chapels are, with a small number of exceptions, in the ownership of the Crown rather than religious bodies and the power to make regulations under subsection (5) provides the flexibility to accommodate the specific circumstances of these chapels in England and Wales. Any such regulations must be made by the affirmative procedure.

The Marriage (Registrar General's Licence) Act 1970
Section 7 – Opt-in: "deathbed marriages"

Section 7 amends section 1 of the Marriage (Registrar General's Licence) Act 1970 so that the Registrar General can only authorise a religious marriage ceremony of a same sex couple if the relevant governing authority has consented to marriages of same sex couples. The circumstances in which the Registrar General may authorise a marriage are where one of the couple is seriously ill, for example in a hospital or at home, is not expected to recover and cannot be moved. Marriages according to the rites of the Church of England or the Church in Wales cannot be authorised under section 1 of the Marriage (Registrar General's Licence) Act 1970 so these provisions do not apply to the Church of England or Church in Wales. This section will allow same sex couples to have "deathbed marriages" according to the rites of religious organisations which have opted in to the solemnization of marriages of same sex couples. Civil marriage ceremonies of same sex couples do not require the consent of any governing authority and so can proceed under section 1 of the Marriage (Registrar General's Licence) Act 1970.

The Church in Wales
Section 8 – Power to allow for marriage of same sex couples in Church in Wales

Section 8 sets out a procedure by which the Church in Wales can choose to allow marriages of same sex couples to take place according to its rites. Should the Governing Body of the Church in Wales resolve that the law should be changed to enable this to happen, it may request that the Lord Chancellor make an order to enable it to do so. Having received such a request, the Lord Chancellor must make an order enabling this to be achieved. In making the order, the Lord Chancellor must have regard to the terms of that resolution, and the order can amend England and Wales legislation (e.g. the Marriage Act) if necessary.

The Church in Wales is in broadly the same position as the Church of England as regards marriage law despite the disestablishment of the Church in Wales by virtue of the Welsh Church Act 1914. However, this disestablishment means that the Church in Wales is not itself able to put legislation before Parliament (unlike the Church of England). The power in this section is therefore required so that the law can be changed to allow the Church in Wales to marry same sex couples (if it were to resolve to allow this) without the need for primary legislation. An order under this section is subject to the affirmative procedure.

Other provisions relating to marriages of same sex couples
Section 9 – Conversion of civil partnership into marriage

Section 9(1) enables civil partners who had their partnership formed in England and Wales to have their partnership converted into a marriage, and provides a power for the Secretary of State to make regulations establishing the procedures for doing so.

Subsections (2) and (3) provide a power for the Secretary of State to make regulations establishing procedures for conversion of civil partnerships formed outside the United Kingdom under an Order in Council made under Chapter 1 of Part 5 of the Civil Partnership Act which deals with civil partnerships registered at British consulates or by armed forces personnel. Subsection (3) makes clear that this applies where England and Wales is the relevant part of the United Kingdom for the purposes of registration of the civil partnership under the respective Order. The use of this power is subject to the affirmative parliamentary procedure.

Subsections (4) and (5) set out the scope of the regulation-making powers, including regulations about:

- the application procedure for conversion;
- the information required to support the application;

- declarations to support an application to convert (for example, by the civil partners themselves);

- a requirement for applicants to appear for example before a local registrar or at a register office, in order, for example, to validate their identity;

- conferral of functions in connection with applications to convert on, for example, the Secretary of State, the Registrar General, armed forces personnel, or other persons. These functions include record-keeping; issuing certified copies of records; conducting civil ceremonies or services following conversion into a marriage;
- application fees and fees for connected functions.

Under subsection (6), the completed conversion process automatically ends the civil partnership and the couple are treated as having been married since the date the civil partnership was formed.

Section 10 – Extra-territorial matters

Section 10 provides that existing or new marriages of same sex couples that take place outside England and Wales can be recognised as marriages under the law of England and Wales. It is irrelevant whether the law of the place of marriage provides for marriage of same sex couples before or after this provision comes into force. Section 10 also gives effect to Schedule 2, which contains more detailed provisions (see below). Overseas marriages of opposite sex couples which are valid as to capacity and form according to the relevant law are recognised under the law of England and Wales. New and existing overseas marriages of same sex couples which are valid as to capacity and form according to the relevant law will be recognised under the law of England and Wales from the date of implementation of the Act.

Effect of extension of marriage
Section 11 – Effect of extension of marriage

Section 11(1) provides that, as a result of the extension of marriage to same sex couples, marriage has the same effect in law in relation to such a couple as it does in relation to an opposite sex couple. Section 11(2) ensures that the law of England and Wales, including all existing and new England and Wales legislation, will be interpreted in this way. Subsection (3) brings into effect Schedule 3, which provides specific provision for interpretation of existing legislation (Part 1) and new legislation (Part 2). Section 11(1) and (2) with Schedule 3 together set out the equivalence of all marriages in law.

There are some circumstances in which the effect which would be obtained by the application of section 11 needs to be clarified or where it is not to apply. So subsection (4) brings into effect Schedule 4 which provides separately for the effect of the extension of marriage in particular cases and contains a power (Part 7) to make provision that is contrary to the provisions in subsections (1) and (2) of this section, section 9(6)(b) of the Act, and Schedule 3.

Subsection (6) provides that the equivalence provisions of this section and Schedule 3 do not affect Measures and Canons, subordinate legislation, or other ecclesiastical law of the Church of England, ensuring that in Church of England law "marriage" will continue to mean only marriage of a man with a woman.

****

Part 2

Section 12 – Change of gender of married persons or civil partners

Section 12 brings into effect Schedule 5 (Change of gender of married persons or civil partners). Part 1 of Schedule 5 amends the Gender Recognition Act 2004 to enable couples in "protected marriages" to remain married following one or both parties obtaining gender recognition, if both parties to the marriage wish the marriage to continue. Part 2 of Schedule 5 amends the Gender Recognition Act 2004 to enable applicants who were or who are currently in protected marriages and who started living in their acquired gender a long time ago to apply for gender recognition under a modified medical evidence procedure.

Section 13 – Marriage overseas

Section 13 brings into effect Schedule 6 (Marriage overseas) and repeals the Foreign Marriage Act 1892 for England and Wales, and Scotland. The Orders in Council that may be made under Schedule 6 will replace the provision currently made by the Foreign Marriage Act 1892 for marriages for both same sex and opposite sex couples.

Section 14 – Marriages according to the usages of belief organisations

Section 14(1) requires the Secretary of State to arrange for a review of whether an order should be made permitting belief organisations to solemnize marriages and to consider what provision should be made in the order. Subsection (7) defines a belief organisation as an organisation whose principal or sole purpose is the advancement of a system of non-religious beliefs which relate to morality or ethics.

Under subsections (2) and (3), the arrangements for the review must provide for a full public consultation and the Secretary of State must arrange for a report on the outcome of the review to be produced and published by 1 January 2015. Subsection (4) gives the Secretary of State the power to make provision by order permitting marriages according to the usages of belief organisations. The exercise of this power is subject to the affirmative parliamentary procedure. Under subsection (5), such an order may amend any England and Wales legislation (both primary and secondary legislation), and may make provision for the charging of fees. In accordance with subsection (6), such an order must also provide that there can be no religious element in a marriage ceremony under the order.

Section 15 – Review of civil partnership

Section 15 requires the Secretary of State to arrange for a review to be carried out on the operation and future of the Civil Partnership Act in England and Wales. The review must begin as soon as practicable and must include a full public consultation. A report on the outcome of the review must be published.

Subsection (2) provides that the review can look at other matters relating to civil partnerships.

Section 16 – Survivor benefits under occupational pension schemes

Section 16 requires the Secretary of State to arrange for a review to be carried out on relevant differences in survivor benefits in occupational pension schemes. The review must consider differences between: same sex survivor benefits and opposite sex survivor benefits provided to widows; same sex survivor benefits and opposite sex survivor benefits provided to widowers; opposite sex survivor benefits provided to widows; and opposite sex survivor benefits provided to widowers. The review must consider what the costs and other effects would be if the relevant differences in survivor benefits were eliminated. In particular the review must consider the extent to which occupational pension schemes provide survivor benefits relying on the exception in paragraph 18 of Schedule 9 to the Equality Act 2010 (which provides that it is not unlawful sexual orientation discrimination for an occupational pension scheme not to provide benefits to the surviving partner of a civil partnership, in respect of pension rights accrued by the deceased partner prior to 5 December 2005); and the extent to which same sex survivor benefits and opposite sex survivor benefits are calculated by reference to different periods of pensionable service. The review must include consultation with interested parties whom the Secretary of State considers appropriate, and a report of the review must be published before 1 July 2014. If the Secretary of State, having considered the outcome of the review, thinks that the law should be changed in order to eliminate or reduce differences in survivor benefits, subsection (6) sets out that provision may be made in an order subject to approval by Parliament by the affirmative parliamentary procedure.

****

Part 3 – Final provisions

Section 17 – Transitional and consequential provision

It may be necessary to deal with the transition from the situation where marriage is only available to opposite sex couples to the situation where marriage is also available to same sex couples. It may also be necessary to deal with the consequences of that change. Section 17 provides powers for the Secretary of State or Lord Chancellor to make orders that would allow these sorts of circumstances to be dealt with:

- transitional, transitory or saving provision in connection with the coming into force of any provision of the Act may be made under subsection (1);

- provision in consequence of the Act may be made under subsection (2).

Under subsection (3), any such order may include amendments to primary or subordinate legislation of any part of the United Kingdom. If the order makes amendments to primary legislation it must be made by the affirmative parliamentary procedure; otherwise the power is subject to the negative procedure.

Subsection (4) brings into effect Schedule 7 (Transitional and consequential provision etc).

Section 18 – Orders and regulations

This section sets out the arrangements for how Ministers are to exercise their delegated powers. Section 18 determines which powers, exercisable by the Secretary of State or Lord Chancellor under the Act, require which parliamentary procedure:

- affirmative procedure is required for:

- an order under section 8 and paragraph 9(8) of Schedule 6 to allow marriage of same sex couples according to the rites of the Church in Wales;

- regulations made for the first time under section 9 setting out arrangements for the conversion of civil partnerships;

- an order under section 14;

- an order under section 16;

- an order amending an Act of Parliament under section 17(1) or (2);

- an order under paragraph 1(1) of Schedule 2, which provides for a marriage of a same sex couple under the law of England and Wales to be treated as a civil partnership in Scotland, or an order made under paragraph 1(2) modifying or disapplying the provisions of an order made under paragraph 1(1);

- an order under paragraph 2 of Schedule 2 modifying or disapplying the effect of paragraph 2(1) (which provides that marriages of same sex couples are treated as civil partnerships under the law of Northern Ireland);

- an order under paragraph 27 of Schedule 4, to make contrary provisions to the general proposition in the Act which makes marriage in law have the same effect in relation to marriages of same sex couples as it does for marriages of opposite sex couples

Negative procedure is applied for;

- regulations under section 9 making provision in relation to the conversion of civil partnership into marriage, other than on the first exercise of this power;

- an order under section 17(1) or (2) which does not amend an Act of Parliament.

Subsection (4) provides for orders and regulations under the Act to make different provision for different purposes; and to make transitional, transitory, saving or consequential provision.

Subsection (5) enables the Secretary of State to delegate the making of certain regulations to the Registrar General, but only where the regulations are to be made under section 9 (Conversion of civil partnership to marriage) or under section 14(4) (in relation to marriage by belief organisations).

Subsection (6) provides that such provision may not enable the Registrar General to require a fee to be paid or set the amount for such a fee. The Secretary of State may not delegate his or her regulation-making power to the Registrar General unless he or she is satisfied that it is needed in connection with the administrative functions of the Registrar General.

Subsections (7) and (8) provide that the default parliamentary procedure for regulations made by the Registrar General is the negative procedure, but the Secretary of State may make alternative provision in the order made under subsection (5).

Subsection (10) provides that the power to amend legislation by secondary legislation includes the power to repeal or revoke legislation.

Subsection (11) requires the Secretary of State or Lord Chancellor to obtain the consent of the Scottish Ministers or the Department of

Finance and Personnel in Northern Ireland before making any orders or regulations amending legislation within the devolved areas of competence of the Scottish Parliament or the Northern Ireland Assembly.

Section 19 – Interpretation

Section 19 defines various expressions used in the Act:
"primary legislation",

"subordinate legislation",

"England and Wales legislation",

"Northern Ireland legislation",

"Scottish legislation",

"UK legislation",

"existing England and Wales legislation",

"new England and Wales legislation",

"registrar",

"Registrar General"

"superintendent registrar".

Section 20 – Extent

The extent of the Act's provisions is primarily covered in paragraph 16 above. In addition, amendments, revocations or repeals made by the Act have the same extent as the provision being amended, revoked or

repealed. Any amendments to the Social Security Contributions and Benefits Act 1992, the Pension Schemes Act 1993, the Human Fertilisation and Embryology Act 2008 and the review of civil partnership only extend to England and Wales.
Section 21 – Short title and commencement

82. Sections 15, 16 and 21 came into force on 17 July 2013 - the day on which the Act received Royal Assent. Any other provision will come into force by order of the Secretary of State.
Schedule 1 – Registration of buildings etc
Introduction

Schedule 1 inserts provisions into the Marriage Act to deal with the details of registering certified places of worship for marriage of same sex couples according to religious rites and usages; appointing authorised persons for that purpose; and cancelling registration, along with powers for the Registrar General to make further detailed procedural regulations.

Registration of buildings
Paragraph 2 of Schedule 1 ("Registration of buildings") inserts new sections 43A to 43D into the Marriage Act.

New section 43A deals with the procedures for registration of buildings as places where same sex couples can get married. This can be additional to, or separate from, registration as a place where a man and a woman can get married.
As with registration under section 41 (for marriages between a man and a woman), a building cannot be registered for marriage of same sex couples unless it has been certified as a place of worship (subsection (1)). Part of a building may be registered (subsection (6)).

The application is made, as with applications to register a building for marriage of opposite sex couples, by the proprietor or trustee of the building to the superintendent registrar for the local registration district (subsection (2)).

The application must be accompanied by a certificate demonstrating the consent of the relevant governing authority, a copy of that consent and (if the building is not already registered for marriage (of opposite sex couples) under section 41 of the Marriage Act), a certificate of use for religious worship (subsection (3)). Certificate of use for religious worship is defined in subsection (7); it must be dated not earlier than one month before the application is made and must be signed by at least twenty householders who are members of the regular congregation who want the building to be used as a place for same sex couples to get married.

The local registrar must send the application with the certificates to the Registrar General, who must register the building (subsections (4) and (5)).

New section 43B deals with the appointment of authorised persons for the purpose of marriages of same sex couples. There are already authorised persons for marriages of opposite sex couples: for example, a warden, verger or other church official (he or she could be, but is not normally, a member of the clergy) who is appointed by the local church to keep its marriage register and to be present at the marriage and ensure the marriage certificate is signed and an entry made in the marriage register on behalf of the local registrar. There does not have to be an authorised person for each registered building, but if there is not, the registrar must be present at the marriage and ensure the certificates are signed and an entry made in the register.

New section 43B enables the trustees or governing body of the religious building to appoint an authorised person for marriages of same sex couples (subsection (1)) and, if they do so, requires that they inform the Registrar General and local superintendent registrar (subsection (2)). This is the same process as for religious marriage ceremonies currently. If there is already an authorised person for the building, it will be open to the governing body or trustees to appoint that same person for marriages of same sex couples, or a different person.

Where the building is not already registered under section 41, authorised persons can only be appointed after one year following registration under new section 43A, so as to enable the registrar to oversee the initial transition to solemnizing and registering marriages (subsections (3) to (6)). This also applies to new registrations under section 41, where the building is not already registered under new section 43A.

Quakers (Society of Friends) and people professing the Jewish religion can carry out marriages in places that are not registered. Therefore they do not now, and will not under the Act, need to appoint authorised persons (subsection (8)).

New section 43C enables a building's registration for the conduct of marriages of same sex couples to be cancelled. The procedure for doing so is similar to that for applying for registration. Under subsection (4) of new section 43C, where a building is shared new sections 44A to 44C of the Marriage Act (inserted by paragraph 3 of this Schedule) apply and enable a religious organisation to cancel its registration without the agreement of other sharers.

New section 43D gives the Secretary of State a power to make further regulations regarding the procedures to be followed for applications to register buildings for marriages of same sex couples, applications for the registration of buildings to solemnize marriages of both same sex and opposite sex couples, the procedures for appointment of authorised persons and the cancellation of registrations, including procedures to be followed by superintendent registrars and for payment of fees. The use of this power will be subject to the negative parliamentary procedure.

Shared buildings

Paragraph 3 ("Shared buildings") inserts new sections 44A to 44D into the Marriage Act. New section 44A sets out procedures for the registration for the purpose of religious marriage ceremonies of same sex couples of certified places of worship which are shared between more than one religious organisation under a formal sharing arrangement under the Sharing of Church Buildings Act 1969 or otherwise covered by that Act (such as university or hospital chapels). In particular, section 44A provides that agreement to registration is required from the governing authority of each of the organisations which share the building. All the sharing organisations do not need to consent to solemnize marriages of same sex couples themselves, but need to agree to the building being used to solemnize such marriages. A power is included for the Secretary of State to make regulations in relation to this section.

New section 44B provides for the cancellation of the registration for the conduct of marriages of same sex couples of buildings shared under a formal sharing arrangement. Any application for cancellation must be made in accordance with new section 43C but can be made either by the proprietor or trustee of the building or by the governing authority of any of the sharing churches. If the application is made by a governing authority, it must be accompanied by a written confirmation that the organisation making the application is the relevant governing authority of that religion. The consent of all sharing churches is not required. A power is included for the Secretary of State to make regulations in relation to this section.

New section 44C contains a power for the Secretary of State to make regulations about the registration, cancellation of registration and use of certified places of worship which are used by more than one religious organisation but are not subject to a formal sharing arrangement under, or otherwise dealt with in, the Sharing of Church Buildings Act 1969.

New section 44D provides definitions of terms used in sections 44A to 44C such as "sharing agreement" and "shared building". It also provides power for the Secretary of State to make regulations about the registration of shared buildings, and the use of shared premises for marriage of same sex couples more generally. In particular, the regulations may deal with the solemnization of marriages by Quakers or marriages according to the Jewish religion in shared buildings (including consents for registration and cancellation of registrations in these cases). Under subsection (8) of this new section, the affirmative procedure is required for use of any of the powers relating to shared buildings.

Schedule 2 – Extra-territorial matters
Part 1 – English and Welsh marriages of same sex couples: treatment in Scotland and Northern Ireland

Paragraph 1 gives the Secretary of State a power to make an order, after obtaining the consent of the Scottish Ministers, to provide that marriages of same sex couples solemnized under the law of England and Wales are to be treated under the law of Scotland as civil partnerships. This power could be used in the event that, when marriage of same sex couples becomes lawful in England and Wales, it is not lawful in Scotland. Without legal recognition of their status, a same sex couple who married in London, for example, and subsequently moved to Glasgow would not be recognised as being in any legal relationship.

The Secretary of State may also make a supplementary order to vary or undo this treatment as a civil partnership in particular circumstances. An order for treating marriages of same sex couples solemnized in England and Wales as civil partnerships cannot be made if marriage of same sex couples has become lawful in Scotland. However, an order that has been made will continue to be valid even if marriage of same sex couples becomes lawful in Scotland, though at that point the order could be revoked. This means that couples treated as civil partners during the period between this Act coming into force and any Scottish legislation coming into force would not retrospectively lose rights acquired as civil partners during that period. Any order made under the Act which would otherwise be within the legislative competence of the Scottish Parliament will be subject to the consent of Scottish Ministers.

Paragraph 2 provides that marriages of a same sex couples solemnized under the law of England and Wales are to be treated under the law of Northern Ireland as civil partnerships. This is to deal with the situation that, though marriage of same sex couples will be lawful in England and Wales, it is not lawful in Northern Ireland. Without legal recognition of their status, a same sex couple who married in London, for example, and subsequently moved to Belfast would not be recognised as being in any legal relationship.

The Secretary of State may also make a supplementary order to vary or undo this treatment as a civil partnership in particular circumstances. Any order made by the Secretary of State or Lord Chancellor under the Act which would otherwise be within the legislative competence of the Northern Ireland Assembly will be subject to the consent of the Department of Finance and Personnel.

Part 2 – Marriage treated as civil partnership: dissolution, annulment or separation

Paragraph 4 provides that where a marriage of a same sex couple is treated as a civil partnership in Scotland or in Northern Ireland and the civil partnership is subsequently dissolved or annulled or an order is made for the separation of the civil partners, then the marriage itself will also automatically be ended or the parties will have a judicial separation under the law of England and Wales.

Part 3 – England and Wales: "overseas relationships" in Civil Partnership Act 2004

Part 5 of the Civil Partnership Act defines the term "overseas relationship" and sets out the circumstances in which a same sex couple who have registered a marriage or civil union overseas are to be treated as having formed a civil partnership under UK law. Paragraph 5 takes into account the fact that the Act makes marriage of same sex couples possible in England and Wales and as a consequence overseas marriages of same sex couples will be treated as marriages under the law of England and Wales.

Schedule 3 – Interpretation of legislation

102.Schedule 3 makes further provision about interpretation of references to marriages in existing (Part 1) and new (Part 2) legislation in England and Wales, in accordance with the principle set out in section 11 that marriage in law has the same effect in relation to same sex couples as to opposite sex couples.

Part 1 – Existing England and Wales legislation

Part 1 sets out details of how particular terms used in existing legislation in England and Wales are to be read once marriage of same couples becomes possible. The particular terms mentioned in paragraph 1 are references to a marriage, a married couple or married person in existing legislation in England and Wales; these are to be read as also referring to a marriage of a same sex couple, married same sex couples or to a person married to someone of the same sex.

Under paragraph 1(2), such references are also to be read across to, for example, cases where a marriage has ended. A reference to a person as a widow would be read as including a reference to a woman whose marriage to another woman ended with the other woman's death, for example.

Paragraph 1(3) ensures that existing England and Wales legislation will be interpreted in accordance with paragraphs 1(1) and (2) no matter what language it uses in making reference to any of the relevant concepts.

Paragraph 2 particularly deals with references to couples living together as if married; these are to be read as also referring to a person who is living with someone of the same sex as if they are married.

Paragraph 3 deals with legislation where there is existing provision which deals differently with a man and a woman living together as if married, and a same sex couple living together as if civil partners. The effect of this paragraph is to preserve the current effect for same sex couples despite the introduction of marriage of same sex couples. In other words, the current distinction is maintained by which an unmarried opposite sex couple are treated as if married, while an unmarried same sex couple not in a civil partnership are treated as if in a civil partnership.

Paragraph 4 ensures that the terms specified in Part 1 of Schedule 3 are not the only terms whose meaning will change once marriage of same sex couples becomes possible.

Section 144(4) of the Adoption and Children Act 2002 defines the meaning of "a couple" for the purposes of that Act:

> "In this Act, a couple means –
>
> (a) a married couple, or
> (aa) two people who are civil partners of each other, or
> (b) two people (whether of different sexes or the same sex) living as partners in an enduring family relationship.".

Paragraph 1(1)(b) allows for the reference here to a married couple now to include a married same sex couple.

Section 2(1) of the Offices, Shops and Railway Premises Act 1963 as amended states that: "This Act shall not apply to any premises to which it would, apart from this subsection, apply, if none of the persons employed to work in the premises is other than the husband, wife, civil partner ......of the person by whom they are so employed." The terms "husband" and "wife" here refer to a person who is married for the purposes of paragraph 1(1)(c) of Schedule 3. This means that "husband" here will be read as including a man or a woman in a marriage of a same sex couple, as well as a man married to a woman. In a similar way, "wife" will be read as including a woman married to another woman or a man married to a man. The result is that this section is to be read as including both male and female spouses in marriages of same sex couples.

Part 2 – New England and Wales legislation

Part 2 governs how new legislation made after the passing of this Act is to be interpreted. It sets out the meanings of specific words relating to marriage (such as "husband" and "wife"). It reflects the main principle of the Act, which is to put marriage of same sex couples on an equal footing with marriage of opposite sex couples. This will ensure that gender-specific terms such as "husband" keep their gender-specific effect.

It should be noted that in Part 7 of Schedule 4, paragraph 27 provides a power for the Secretary of State to modify or disapply the provisions of Schedule 3 in specified circumstances.

Schedule 4 – Effect of extension of marriage: further provision
Part 1 – Private legal instruments

This provision means that the introduction of marriage of same sex couples will not affect the meaning of any marriage-related reference in documents, such as wills, deeds and documents governing charities, drawn up prior to section 11 coming into force. Such references will be understood only in terms of marriage of opposite sex couples.

In future, after this Act comes into force, a reference to marriage in any new document may be understood as including marriage of same sex couples (depending on the precise terminology of the document).

Part 2 – Presumption on birth of child to married woman

Paragraph 2 makes clear that the common law presumption, that a child born to a woman during her marriage is also the child of her husband (often referred to as "the presumption of legitimacy"), is not extended to marriages of same sex couples by section 11. Therefore, where two women are married to each other and one of the parties to that marriage gives birth to a child, the other party will not be presumed to be the parent of that child by virtue of the common law presumption. There may be other ways in which the party to the marriage who does not give birth to the child is treated in law as the parent (for example, if that woman is treated as a parent as a result of the amendment made by paragraph 40 of Schedule 7 to this Act to section 42 of the Human Fertilisation and Embryology Act 2008), but in all such cases it is not the common law presumption that treats her as the parent of that child.

Part 3 – Divorce and annulment of marriage

Paragraph 3 adds a new subsection 1(6) in the Matrimonial Causes Act 1973. Section 1 of that Act sets out various facts for proving that a marriage has broken down irretrievably (the ground for divorce), including in subsection 1(2) (a) that one of the parties to the marriage has committed adultery and the other finds it intolerable to live with that party. New subsection 1(6) maintains the existing definition of adultery and provides that only conduct between one party to the marriage and a person of the opposite sex may constitute adultery. This applies to both opposite sex and same sex couples.

Paragraph 4 amends section 12 of the Matrimonial Causes Act 1973. The effect of this amendment is that non-consummation (either by reason of incapacity or wilful refusal) cannot be a ground on which a marriage of a same sex couple is voidable. The provisions for opposite sex couples remain unaltered.

Part 4 – Matrimonial proceedings

Same sex couples who marry in England and Wales but remain or become habitually resident or domiciled in another country may not be able to end their marriage in that country if it does not recognise the existence of the relationship. Part 4 therefore amends the Domicile and Matrimonial Proceedings Act 1973 to provide a "jurisdiction of last resort" so that those same sex couples who are unable to divorce or obtain other matrimonial orders in the country which would normally have jurisdiction are able to have their case heard in the courts in England and Wales. "Jurisdiction" means a court's authority to deal with the case. The courts in England and Wales will be able to assume jurisdiction if the couple were married in England or Wales and where it is the interests of justice to do so.

Paragraph 6 amends section 5 of the Domicile and Matrimonial Proceedings Act 1973 to set out which provisions in respect of jurisdiction in matrimonial causes do not apply to marriages of same sex couples, which are instead dealt with in Schedule A1. It also amends section 5 to provide that Schedule 1 to the Domicile and Matrimonial Proceedings Act 1973, which relates to stays of proceedings, will apply to marriages of opposite sex and same sex couples. Paragraph 7 amends section 6 of that Act to insert reference to Schedule A1. Paragraph 8 inserts Schedule A1 to that Act. Paragraph 1 of Schedule A1 sets out the jurisdiction of the court in proceedings for orders relating to the ending of a marriage (divorce, judicial separation, nullity of marriage or because one of the couple is dead) and orders relating to declarations of validity.

Paragraph 2 of Schedule A1 provides that the court is able to deal with divorce, judicial separation and nullity cases either (a) where the court has jurisdiction because of regulations made under paragraph 5 of Schedule A1 (see below), or (b) when no court has that jurisdiction and either of the married same sex couple is domiciled in England and Wales when the case starts, or (c) when the same sex couple married under the law of England and Wales, no court has the paragraph 5 jurisdiction and it appears to the court in the interests of justice for it to deal with the case. In nullity cases the court additionally has jurisdiction if either of the couple died before the case started and was domiciled in England and Wales on the date of death or had been habitually resident in England and Wales throughout the year ending with the date of death.

The court also has jurisdiction to deal with divorce, judicial separation or nullity for the same marriage when proceedings are pending under sub-paragraphs (1) or (2).

Paragraph 3 of Schedule A1 provides that the court has jurisdiction to deal with an application by one of a couple for an order which ends their marriage on the ground that their spouse is dead, provided that at the time the application was made the High Court did not have jurisdiction under the Presumption of Death Act 2013 to hear an application for a declaration that the applicant's spouse is presumed dead, the two people concerned married under the law of England and Wales and it appears to the court to be in the interests of justice to deal with the case.

Paragraph 4 of Schedule A1 says the court has jurisdiction to deal with an application for a declaration of validity if either party to the marriage concerned is domiciled in England and Wales on the date the case starts, was habitually resident in England and Wales throughout the year before the date the case starts, or died before that date and at death was either domiciled in England and Wales or had been habitually resident in England and Wales throughout the year ending with the date of death, or the two people concerned married under the law of England and Wales and it appears to the court to be in the interests of justice to deal with the case.

Paragraph 5 of Schedule A1 enables the Lord Chancellor to make regulations about the jurisdiction of the courts to deal with divorce, judicial separation and nullity cases and about the recognition of such orders for a married same sex couple. These regulations would apply where one of the couple: is or has been habitually resident in a Member State of the European Union (EU), or is an EU national, or is domiciled in a part of the UK or the Republic of Ireland. The regulations may correspond with the terms of Council Regulation (EC) No 2201/2003 (known as Brussels IIa) on jurisdiction, recognition and enforcement of judgments in matrimonial matters and in matters of parental responsibility. Brussels IIa deals with marriage of opposite sex couples. The provisions on recognition of judgments can apply retrospectively. A statutory instrument containing these regulations will be subject to the affirmative resolution procedure.

Paragraph 6 of Schedule A1 sets out the meaning of "declaration of validity" in that Schedule as: a declaration as to the validity of a marriage, a declaration as to whether a marriage existed on a particular date, or a declaration as to the validity of matrimonial orders obtained outside England and Wales.

Paragraph 10 of Schedule 4 to the Act makes transitory provision to ensure that the provisions on the court's jurisdiction to hear presumption of death proceedings will function under section 19 of the Matrimonial Causes Act 1973 if this Act were to come into force before the entry into force of the Presumption of Death Act 2013 and until the Presumption of Death Act 2013 comes into force.
Part 5 – State pensions

Part 5 makes provision about a person's entitlement to state pension based on a current or deceased spouse's or civil partner's National Insurance record. This entitlement is payable by way of a "Category B pension" under the Social Security Contributions and Benefits Act 1992.

Under section 48A of that Act, a married person or civil partner may be entitled to a lower-rate basic state pension based on the spouse's or civil partner's National Insurance record while the spouse or partner is alive, and up to a full basic pension and a proportion of the spouse's or civil partner's additional (earnings-related) state pension after their death. However, for married men and civil partners, entitlement is restricted to those whose wives or partners were born on or after 6 April 1950. Paragraph 11(1) replicates this restriction for a person who is married to a person of the same sex. However, paragraph 11(2) provides that the restriction does not apply to a woman married to another woman whose spouse was her husband immediately before obtaining a gender recognition certificate. In this situation, she would retain entitlement to state pension based on her spouse's National Insurance contributions, even if the latter was born before 6 April 1950. Paragraph 11(3) amends subsection (2ZA) of the Social Security Contributions and Benefits Act 1992, which defines which contribution condition the person's spouse is required to satisfy depending on when he or she reaches state pension age. The amendment clarifies that the condition applicable to a person who reached state pension age before 6 April 2010 can be relevant only where the spouse is a man married to a woman or (as provided by new (2ZA) and (2ZB)) had been born a man who would have reached pension age in her birth gender before that date.

Under section 48B of the Social Security Contributions and Benefits Act 1992, a spouse or civil partner who is widowed over state pension age(1) may be entitled to a Category B pension comprising basic pension plus a proportion of the deceased's additional (earnings-related) state pension. Widowers and surviving civil partners cannot qualify under this provision if they reached state pension age before 6 April 2010. Instead, they may qualify under section 51 (see below), provided their late wife or partner died when also over state pension age. The practical effect of this restriction is now limited to instances where the widower or surviving civil partner reached state pension age before 6 April 2010 and the deceased spouse or partner dies while still under state pension age. The restriction, in relation to widowers, is made by paragraph 3(3) of Schedule 4 to the Pensions Act 1995, which will be read as applying to widowers of marriages of same sex couples by virtue of section 11 of this Act. Paragraph 12(1) of Schedule 4 applies an equivalent restriction to women married to women. However, paragraph 12(2) exempts from this restriction women whose female spouses were formerly their husbands. Paragraph 12(3) makes provision corresponding to that made by paragraph 11(3) relating to the applicable contribution condition to be met by the deceased spouse.

As noted in the previous paragraph, section 51 of the Social Security Contributions and Benefits Act 1992 provides a Category B pension for a widower or surviving civil partner who reached state pension age before 6 April 2010 and is widowed when both members of the couple are over state pension age. Section 51 does not apply to widowers or civil partners who reach pension age on or after 6 April 2010, as that entitlement is picked up by either section 48A or 48B. Paragraph 13(2) of Schedule 4 inserts a new subsection (1ZA) into section 51 of that Act, which extends it to include the surviving spouse of a marriage of a same sex couple, so that it may provide a Category B pension where the survivor's pension age is before 6 April 2010 and both are over pension age at the date of widowhood. Paragraph 13(5) and (6) provide that this does not apply to surviving spouses who reached pension age on or after 6 April 2010 or to women whose female spouses were formerly their husbands as they will qualify under either section 48A or 48B.

Apart from the above elements of derived entitlements, a surviving spouse or civil partner may also be entitled to half the deceased's graduated retirement benefit (GRB) – a form of earnings-related pension that could be accrued between 1961 and 1975. Widowers and surviving civil partners who reached state pension age before 6 April 2010 may inherit GRB only if both parties are over state pension age when the spouse or civil partner dies. The provisions for GRB inheritance are in section 37 of the National Insurance Act 1965. Section 62 of the Social Security Contributions and Benefits Act 1992 provides the powers to amend the GRB provisions. Paragraph 14(2) of

Schedule 4 inserts new powers into section 62 to enable regulations to be made extending section 37 of the National Insurance Act 1965 to men and their late husbands and to women and their late wives on the same terms as currently apply to widowers and surviving civil partners. Subsections (3) and (4) have the effect that a woman who was married to a transsexual woman remains entitled to half the GRB of the deceased without restriction – as if her spouse had not changed legal gender.

Adult dependency increases (ADIs) are an increase of state pension that could be awarded under sections 83 to 85 of the Social Security Contributions and Benefits Act 1992 and may be payable to a man in respect of a dependent wife; a wife in respect of a dependent husband; or a person in respect of another adult (not their spouse) who has the care of the pensioner's dependent child. ADIs were abolished from 6 April 2010, but people who were already entitled to an ADI before that date continue to receive it under transitional rules. Under the changes which the Act introduces, a married couple will be able to remain married when one member changes their legal gender. Paragraph 15 provides that an adult dependency increase continues to be payable where the parties to the marriage are still married but no longer husband and wife.

Paragraph 16 provides that where a couple have converted their civil partnership to a marriage under section 9 of the Act, this cannot give rise to entitlement to state pension by virtue of being treated as married in the period preceding the conversion.

Part 6 – Occupational pensions and survivor benefits

Paragraph 18 of Schedule 9 to the Equality Act 2010 provides that it is not discrimination because of sexual orientation to restrict access to a benefit, facility or service that would be available to a person who was married to someone who is in a civil partnership, in relation to rights accrued before 5 December 2005 (the date the Civil Partnership Act came into force). This means that an occupational pension scheme as a minimum only has to provide survivor benefits to civil partners on rights accrued since that date. Paragraph 17 removes the word "married" from sub-paragraph (1) and inserts a new sub-paragraph (1A) into paragraph 18 of Schedule 9 to the Equality Act 2010. This extends the exception so that it also applies to same sex couples in the same way as to civil partners. Sub-paragraph (1A)(c) and (1B) provide that this does not apply to people who were in a marriage with a person of the opposite sex but who are now in a marriage of a same sex couple as a result of one spouse changing legal gender.

Widows and widowers of marriages of same sex couples will be entitled to any guaranteed minimum pension accrued after April 1988. However, an exception is made for a woman in a marriage of a same sex couple whose spouse was her husband immediately before obtaining a gender recognition certificate - a "relevant gender change case". In such cases widows will be treated like widows of men for the purpose of inheritance of the guaranteed minimum pension.

Schemes may convert members' rights to a guaranteed minimum pension into an ordinary scheme pension. Under section 24D of the Pension Schemes Act 1993, the scheme must provide post-conversion benefits that include survivors' benefits. Paragraph 21 amends section 24D to require schemes to provide these survivors' benefits to widows or widowers of marriages of same sex couples. Widows or widowers of marriages of same sex couples will be entitled to the same benefits as surviving civil partners, except as with inheritance of the guaranteed minimum pension where a woman was married to a woman in a relevant gender change case. In these cases a widow will be entitled to a pension of at least half the value of any pension accrued by the earner from April 1978 to April 1997.

Section 37 of the Pension Schemes Act 1993 prohibits alterations to the rules of a contracted-out scheme unless the alteration is of a prescribed description and except in prescribed circumstances. Section 37(3) prohibits such alterations by schemes that were formerly contracted-out so long as any person is entitled to receive benefits for the period when the scheme was contracted-out. Section 37(4) limits the application of section 37(3) where the person entitled is a widower or surviving civil partner to only such cases as may be prescribed. Paragraph 22 amends section 37(4) and inserts new subsections (5) and (6) to extend this limitation to include widows and widowers of marriages of same sex couples except for widows in a relevant gender change case.

In order to benefit from the exception made for relevant gender change cases, widows will need to produce evidence of their spouse having changed legal gender to support their claim. Paragraph 23 inserts new section 38A (Regulations about relevant gender change cases) into the Pension Schemes Act 1993 to enable regulations to be made to specify the detail of what information may need to be provided or other conditions that may be met before schemes are obliged to treat these widows as if they were widows of marriages of opposite sex couples. Under subsection 38A(3) regulations may also specify what schemes must do if the required information is not provided or the conditions are not met for this special exception to apply.

Section 46(1) of the Pension Schemes Act 1993 provides for the reduction of social security benefits where a person is also entitled to a guaranteed minimum pension. Section 47(1) limits the application of section 46(1) in relation to individuals who are entitled to a guaranteed minimum pension by virtue of being the widower or surviving civil partner of an earner in certain circumstances. Section 47(1) does not make any provision about widows, who are currently provided for under section 46(1). The policy intention is that survivors of marriages of same sex couples be treated in the same manner as surviving civil partners in respect of their guaranteed minimum pension entitlement. Paragraph 24 of Schedule 4 gives effect to this policy by making provision for widows of marriages of same sex couples in section 47(1).

Section 84 of the Pension Schemes Act 1993 makes provision about which method of revaluation is to be used to revalue pension benefits.

Subsection (5) is amended by paragraph 25 of Schedule 4 to make reference to the guaranteed minimum of surviving same sex spouses.

Schedule 3 of the Pension Schemes Act 1993 makes further provision about each of the methods of revaluing accrued pension benefits. Paragraph 1(1E) defines "the accrued benefit" for the purposes of paragraph 1, which provides further detail on the final salary method of revaluation. Sub-paragraph (b) is amended by paragraph 26 of Schedule 4 to make reference to the guaranteed minimum of surviving same sex spouses.

Part 7 – Provisions which limit equivalence of all marriages etc

Certain provisions of the Act (referred to in these notes as the "equivalence provisions") have a wide general effect. These provisions are:

- section 11(1) and (2) (which provide for marriage to have the same effect in law in relation to same sex couples that it has in relation to opposite sex couples and for the law of England and Wales to have effect accordingly) and Schedule 3 (which supports section 11(1) and (2) by making specific provision about the interpretation of legislation);

- section 9(6)(b) (which provides that, where a marriage is converted into a civil partnership, the marriage has effect as if it had subsisted since the date when the civil partnership was formed).

In some cases, the wide general effect of the equivalence provisions goes too far, and so would produce results which are not in line with the policy. It is therefore necessary to ensure that the wide general effect of the equivalence provisions does not apply in particular circumstances, or applies in a different way from normal.

Some of these cases are already dealt with in the preceding provisions of Schedule 4. Other cases like this may be dealt with by an order under paragraph 27(3). The legislation which deals with cases like this is referred to as "contrary provision".

Sub-paragraphs 27(1) and (2) ensure that, where cases like this are dealt with by contrary provision, that provision overrides the wide general effect of the equivalence provisions.

Schedule 5 – Change of gender of married persons or civil partners
Part 1

Part 1 of Schedule 5 makes changes to the Gender Recognition Act 2004 (the "Gender Recognition Act"). The Gender Recognition Act enables transsexual people to change their legal gender by applying for a gender recognition certificate under section 1 of that Act. The issue of a full gender recognition certificate enables recipients to be recognised for all legal purposes in their new gender ("the acquired gender"). Under the previous law, transsexual people who are married or in a civil partnership must end their marriage or civil partnership before a full gender recognition certificate can be issued. This is achieved by the Gender Recognition Panel issuing an interim gender recognition certificate to married applicants and applicants in civil partnerships, which causes the marriage or civil partnership to become voidable. Applicants then have six months from the date of issue of the interim gender recognition certificate to apply to the court to end their marriage or civil partnership. Once a marriage or civil partnership has been annulled (or a divorce or dissolution has occurred in Scotland) the court can issue a full gender recognition certificate.

Part 1 of this Schedule amends the Gender Recognition Act to enable an existing marriage registered in England and Wales or outside the UK ("protected marriage" defined in paragraph 14 as a marriage under the law of England and Wales, or a marriage under the law of a country or territory outside the United Kingdom) to continue where one or both parties change their legal gender and both parties wish to remain married. It also amends that Act to enable a civil partnership ("protected civil partnership" defined in paragraph 14 as a civil partnership under the law of England and Wales) to continue where both parties change their legal gender simultaneously and wish to remain in their civil partnership.

Paragraph 2 inserts new subsections (6A), (6B) and (6C) which amend the evidence requirements in section 3 of the Gender Recognition Act. At present, section 3(6)(a) of that Act requires transsexual people who apply to the Gender Recognition Panel for a gender recognition certificate to submit a statutory declaration as to whether they are married or in a civil partnership. This enables the Gender Recognition Panel to determine whether to issue a full gender recognition certificate (for people who are not married or in a civil partnership) or an interim certificate (for people who are married or in a civil partnership).

New subsection (6A) requires married applicants to include in their statutory declaration an additional declaration as to where their marriage was registered. This will enable the Gender Recognition Panel to determine whether the marriage is a protected marriage. Where the marriage is a protected marriage, new subsection (6B) requires an application to contain a declaration by the applicant's spouse that he or she consents to the marriage continuing after the issue of a full gender recognition certificate (a "statutory declaration of consent"), or a statutory declaration by the applicant that his or her spouse has not made such a declaration. If the application contains a statutory declaration of consent by the applicant's spouse, new subsection (6C) requires the Gender Recognition Panel to inform the spouse that an application has been made.

Paragraph 3 replaces existing subsections (2) and (3) of section 4 of the Gender Recognition Act (which provides for the issue of interim and full gender recognition certificates following an application) and inserts new subsections (3A) and (3B) into that section. The effect of these amendments is to enable a full gender recognition certificate to be issued:

- to single applicants (new subsection (2)(a));

- to applicants who are party to a protected marriage and the applicant's spouse has issued a statutory declaration of consent (new subsection (2)(b)); and

- to applicants who are party to a protected civil partnership and the Gender Recognition Panel has decided to issue the other party to the civil partnership with a full gender recognition certificate (new subsection (2)(c)).

Interim gender recognition certificates will be issued:

- to applicants in protected marriages if the applicant's spouse has not consented to the marriage continuing (new subsection (3)(a));

- to applicants in non-protected marriages (new subsection (3)(b));

- to applicants in protected civil partnerships where the other party to the civil partnership has not made an application for a gender recognition certificate at the same time as the applicant, or the other party has made such an application but the Panel has decided not to issue a full gender recognition certificate to him or her (new subsections (3)(c) and (3)(d)); and

- to applicants in non-protected civil partnerships (new subsection (3)(e)).

New subsection (3A) requires the Gender Recognition Panel to notify an applicant's spouse where they issue a full gender recognition certificate to the applicant. New subsection (3B) provides that section 4 of the Gender Recognition Act is subject to new section 5B (inserted into that Act by paragraph 5 of this Schedule).

Paragraph 4 inserts new sections 4A and 4B into the Gender Recognition Act.

New section 4A provides for two situations ("Case A" and "Case B"). Case A provides for the situation where an applicant is in a protected marriage but his or her spouse has not issued a statutory declaration of consent to the marriage continuing. If the applicant's spouse changes his or her mind before the marriage is annulled and wishes the marriage to continue, subsection (2) provides that the applicant can apply to the Gender Recognition Panel for a full gender recognition certificate. The Panel can only issue a full gender recognition certificate to the applicant following such an application if they are satisfied that the following conditions are met:

- an interim gender recognition certificate has been issued to the applicant (subsection (2)(a));

- the applicant was a party to a protected marriage at the time the interim gender recognition certificate was issued (subsection (2)(b));

- the applicant is in a protected marriage (subsection (2)(c)); and

- the applicant's spouse consents to the protected marriage continuing (subsection (2)(d)).

If these conditions are not met, the Gender Recognition Panel will reject an application for a full gender recognition certificate (subsection (4)). Subsection (5) sets a time limit for an application under Case A. The time limit is six months from the date on which the interim certificate was issued.

Case B provides for the situation where an application is made by a civil partner, an interim gender recognition certificate is issued and the couple subsequently decide to convert their civil partnership into a protected marriage under section 9 of this Act. Subsection (3) provides that following a conversion taking place, such applicants can apply for a full gender recognition certificate. The Gender Recognition Panel can only issue a full gender recognition certificate to the applicant if they are satisfied that the following conditions are met:

- an interim gender recognition certificate has been issued to the applicant (subsection (3)(a));

- the applicant was a party to a civil partnership at the time the interim gender recognition certificate was issued (subsection (3)(b));

- the conversion application was made within six months of the date of issue of the interim gender recognition certificate (subsection 3(c));

- the conversion process under section 9 (of this Act) has resulted in the civil partnership being converted into a marriage (subsection (3)(d));

- the applicant is a party to that marriage (subsection (3)(e)); and

- the applicant's spouse consents to the marriage continuing (subsection (3)(f)).

If these conditions are not met, the Gender Recognition Panel will reject an application for a full gender recognition certificate (subsection (4)). Subsection (6) sets a time limit for conversion of an interim gender recognition certificate to a full certificate under this section. The time limit is six months from the date when the civil partnership is converted to a marriage.

Applications under Case A and Case B require the applicant's spouse to issue a statutory declaration of consent to the marriage continuing (subsection (7)). Applications under Case B must additionally include evidence of the date on which the application for conversion under section 9 was made and evidence that the civil partnership has been converted to a marriage (subsection (8)).

Where the Gender Recognition Panel receives an application to issue a full gender recognition certificate in either Case A or Case B, section 4A, subsection (9) requires them to notify the applicant's spouse both of the application and also of the issue of the full gender recognition certificate.

New section 4B provides for the situation where an applicant has made an application for a full gender recognition certificate under new section 4A but before that application can be determined the applicant's spouse dies. Under the previous law, if the applicant's spouse dies within six months of the interim gender recognition certificate being issued, the applicant can apply for a full gender recognition certificate within six months from the date the death occurred (section 5(2)(b) of the Gender Recognition Act). This section may not be available to applicants if the application has not been determined within the time limit in new section 4A(5) and (6). New section 4B provides that in such cases the applicant can still rely on section 5(2)(b) to apply for a full gender recognition certificate.

Paragraph 5 inserts new section 5B into the Gender Recognition Act. If both parties to a protected civil partnership make successful applications to the Gender Recognition Panel, amended section 4(2)(c) of the Gender Recognition Act applies, and both parties will be entitled to full gender recognition certificates. In such cases, new section 5B enables the Gender Recognition Panel to issue full gender recognition certificates to both parties simultaneously, ensuring that the continuity of the civil partnership is not affected by the changes to both parties' legal gender.

Paragraph 6 amends section 6 (Errors in certificates) of the Gender Recognition Act. The amendments provide for the situation where the Gender Recognition Panel or court inadvertently issues the wrong gender recognition certificate or issues a gender recognition certificate with incorrect information. New subsection (1) allows the person covered by the certificate or the Secretary of State to apply to the Gender Recognition Panel or court which issued the certificate to issue the correct certificate or to correct information in the certificate.

Paragraphs 7 and 8 make consequential amendments to section 7 (Applications: supplementary) and section 8 (Appeals etc) of the Gender Recognition Act. Paragraph 8 also inserts new subsection (5A) into section 8 of that Act. New subsection (5A) enables an applicant's spouse to apply to the court where he or she considers that a full gender recognition certificate has been obtained by his or her spouse fraudulently.

Paragraph 9 (1) amends section 10 of the Gender Recognition Act. New subsection (1A) provides that if the Gender Recognition Panel issue full gender recognition certificates to one or both parties in a protected marriage or both parties in a protected civil partnership, the Secretary of State must send a copy of the full gender recognition certificate(s) to the Registrar General for England and Wales.

Paragraph 9(2) amends Part 1 of Schedule 3 to the Gender Recognition Act. New paragraph 11A provides the Registrar General of England and Wales with a power to make regulations about the registration of qualifying marriages and civil partnerships (defined as marriages and civil partnerships registered in England and Wales where one or both parties (both parties in relation to civil partnerships) have been issued with full gender recognition certificates). In particular the regulations may provide for the maintenance of separate marriage and civil partnership registers that record details of qualifying marriages and civil partnerships.

Paragraph 10 inserts new section 11A into the Gender Recognition Act. Subsection (2) provides that, throughout the United Kingdom, the continuity of a protected marriage registered under the law of England and Wales is not affected by the issuing of full gender recognition certificates to one or both of the parties to the marriage. Despite this provision's United Kingdom extent, this provision does not require the law of Scotland or Northern Ireland to recognise such unions as marriages. The provision merely ensures that for the purposes of the law of England and Wales, there is no break in the continuity of marriages registered in England and Wales which continue following one or both parties obtaining gender recognition. Subsection (3)(a) provides that the continuity of a protected marriage registered under the law of a country outside the United Kingdom is not affected by the issuing of full gender recognition certificates to one or both of the parties to the marriage. However, subsection (3)(b) provides that protected marriages registered under the law of a country outside the United Kingdom are still subject to the law of the country in which they are registered, despite being recognised by the law in the United Kingdom whilst the couple are resident there.

Paragraph 11 inserts a new section 11B into the Gender Recognition Act. Section 11B provides that, throughout the United Kingdom, the continuity of a protected civil partnership is not affected by the issuing of full gender recognition certificates to both of the parties to the civil partnership under section 4(2)(c) of that Act.

Paragraph 12 has the effect of disapplying section 21(2) to (5) of the Gender Recognition Act (Foreign gender change and marriage). Section 21(2) to (5) provides for the situation where a transsexual person claims to have changed legal gender in their country of origin and married a person of the opposite sex to their acquired gender in that country or another country outside the UK. At present, these marriages have no standing under the law of England and Wales until a full gender recognition certificate has been issued by the Gender Recognition Panel because the law of the England and Wales regards the parties as having not been respectively male and female when the marriage was solemnized. As marriages in England and Wales will now be available to legally same sex couples, these sections can be disapplied for the purposes of the law of England and Wales.

Paragraph 13 makes a consequential amendment to section 22 of the Gender Recognition Act.

Paragraph 14 inserts the definitions of "protected civil partnership", "protected marriage" and "statutory declaration of consent" into section 25 of the Gender Recognition Act (Interpretation).
Part 2 – Alternative grounds for granting applications for gender recognition certificates

Part 2 of Schedule 5 makes additional changes to the Gender Recognition Act. When the Gender Recognition Act came into force on 4 April 2005, section 27 included a modified evidence process which was open to applicants who could produce evidence that they had been living in their acquired gender for six years prior to the date on which they made their application. The so-called "fast track" process ran for the first two years after commencement of the Gender Recognition Act and expired on 3 April 2007. Part 2 of Schedule 5 inserts a new modified evidence process into the Gender Recognition Act which is not limited in time. The modified evidence process set out in new section 3B of the Gender Recognition Act will only be available to applicants who meet the four conditions set out in new section 3A of the Act.

Paragraph 16 inserts new subsection (3A) into section 2 of the Gender Recognition Act. New subsection (3A) provides that section 2 of the Gender Recognition Act (Determination of applications) does not apply to any application under section 1(1)(a) of the Gender Recognition Act where the applicant indicates that they are making an application for a gender recognition certificate to be granted in accordance with new section 3A of the Gender Recognition Act.

Paragraph 17 inserts new section 3A into the Gender Recognition Act. New section 3A(2) provides that, if the Gender Recognition Panel is satisfied that the applicant meets the four conditions set out in new sections 3A(3) to (6) and has complied with the evidence requirements set out in new section 3B, it must grant the application subject to section 4 of the Gender Recognition Act (Successful applications). If the Gender Recognition Panel is not satisfied, it must reject the application in accordance with new section 3A(7).

New subsections 3A(3) to (6) set out the four conditions applicants must meet to be eligible to rely on the modified evidence process set out in new section 3B of the Gender Recognition Act:

The first condition is that the applicant was a party to a protected marriage or protected civil partnership on or before the date they make their application for gender recognition.

The second condition is that the applicant: was living in their acquired gender for six years prior to the date of commencement of section 12 of the Act; has continued to live in their acquired gender until the date they made their application; and intends to continue living in their acquired gender until death.

The third condition is that the applicant has or has had gender dysphoria or has undergone treatment for the purpose of modifying sexual characteristics.

The fourth condition is that the applicant is ordinarily resident in England, Wales or Scotland.

Paragraph 18 inserts new subsection (9) into section 3 of the Gender Recognition Act which disapplies the evidence requirements set out in section 3 in respect of applications where the applicant indicates that they are making an application for a gender recognition certificate to be issued in accordance with new section 3A of the Gender Recognition Act.

Paragraph 19 inserts new section 3B into the Gender Recognition Act. New section 3B sets out the modified evidence process an applicant who meets the four conditions in new section 3A of the Gender Recognition Act is entitled to rely on.

New subsections 3B(2) to (4) set out medical evidence applicants are required to submit. If the applicant is applying on the basis of having or having had gender dysphoria, a report made by a registered medical practitioner specialising in the field of gender dysphoria or a registered psychologist practising in the field of gender dysphoria which sets out details of the diagnosis of gender dysphoria is required. If the applicant is applying on the basis of having undergone treatment for the purpose of modifying sexual characteristics, or if the applicant indicates that they are currently undergoing such treatment or that such treatment has been planned or prescribed for them, a report made by a registered medical practitioner or registered psychologist practising in the field of gender dysphoria which sets out details of the treatment is required.

New sections 3B(5) to (8) set out the additional evidence applicants are required to submit. New section 3B(5) requires applicants to include a statutory declaration that they meet the conditions in new section 3A of the Gender Recognition Act. New section 3B(6) requires applicants to include in their statutory declaration a declaration as to whether they are single, married or in a civil partnership. The Secretary of State can amend the evidence requirements in new section 3B by order and the Gender Recognition Panel may require applicants to submit any additional evidence it requires to determine the application provided it gives reasons for such requests (new section 3B(10)). Applicants can also submit any additional evidence they wish to include in their application.

If an applicant indicates that they are married, new section 3B(7) requires married applicants or applicants in civil partnerships to include in their statutory declaration an additional declaration as to where their marriage or civil partnership was registered. This will enable the Gender Recognition Panel to determine whether the marriage or civil partnership is a protected marriage or civil partnership. Where the marriage is a protected marriage, new section 3B(8) requires an application to contain a statutory declaration of consent ("statutory declaration of consent" defined in new section 3(6B) of the Gender Recognition Act as "a declaration by the applicant's spouse that he or she consents to the marriage continuing after the issue of a full gender recognition certificate") or a statutory declaration by the applicant that his or her spouse has not made such a declaration. If the application contains a statutory declaration of consent by the applicant's spouse, new section 3B(9) requires the Gender Recognition Panel to inform the spouse that an application has been made.

Paragraph 20 amends Schedule 1 to the Gender Recognition Act to insert new subparagraph (3) to paragraph 4. New paragraph 4(3) provides that the Gender Recognition Panel need not include a medical member when determining any application under section 1(1)(a) of the Gender Recognition Act where the application is for a gender recognition certificate to be granted in accordance with new section 3A of that Act.

Schedule 6 – Marriage overseas

Schedule 6 deals with marriages (including marriages of same sex couples) in British consulates overseas; certificates of no impediment issued to facilitate overseas marriages and civil partnerships carried out under local laws, indicating that no legal impediment has been shown preventing the relevant party from getting married or entering into a civil partnership; and marriages on armed forces bases overseas.

The overall effect of Parts 1 and 2 is to provide a power for Her Majesty by Order in Council to legislate in relation to the arrangements for marriage (including marriage of same sex couples) in overseas consulates and the issuing of certificates of no impediment. The provisions in Parts 1 and 2 largely replicate sections 210 (Registration at British consulates etc), 240 (Certificates of no impediment to overseas relationships) and 244 (Orders in Council: supplementary) of the Civil Partnership Act. The Civil Partnership Act (through the Civil Partnership (Registration Abroad and Certificates) Order 2005), allows the provisions of the Foreign Marriage Act 1892 to be replicated for the purposes of carrying out consular civil partnerships. The effect of Part 3 is to provide for a very similar power for Her Majesty by Order in Council to legislate to enable service personnel and accompanying civilians (including same sex couples) to marry overseas.

Part 1 – Consular marriage under UK law

Paragraph 1(1) provides a power for Her Majesty by Order in Council to make provision for couples to marry in the presence of a registration officer outside the United Kingdom provided that the conditions in sub-paragraph (2) are met.

The conditions in sub-paragraph (2) that must be satisfied in order for a consular marriage to take place are: at least one of the people proposing to marry must be a United Kingdom national; the people proposing to marry would have been eligible to marry in a specified part of the United Kingdom (this caters for a situation where different parts of the United Kingdom allow or do not allow marriage of same sex couples); the authorities of the country or territory in which the consulate is located will not object; and either there are insufficient facilities for them to marry under the law of that country or territory or, in the case of same sex couples, they cannot be married under the law of that country or territory. For example, currently consular marriages are conducted in Saudi Arabia and five other countries in the Middle East, where there are no local facilities and the local authorities have no objection. The United Kingdom government would need to approach host governments in countries where facilities for marriage of same sex couples do not exist to seek their approval to conduct such marriages.

Paragraph 2 allows a consular official to refuse to marry a couple if the officer thinks the marriage would be inconsistent with international law or comity of nations (the mutual respect of one nation for another's usages and practices), although there is a power to provide for an appeal against this decision in the Order in Council referred to in paragraph 1(1). The Order in Council may also include provisions that enable the marriage to be treated as if the couple had been married in the specified part of the United Kingdom for certain purposes.

Part 2 – Marriage under foreign law: certificates of no impediment

Part 2 (paragraph 7) provides a power for Her Majesty by Order in Council to legislate to make provision for the issue of certificates of no impediment to marriage where a United Kingdom national wishes to marry overseas according to local laws if that country or territory is prescribed in the Order in Council. The Act contains a power to extend this to other "prescribed" persons.

Part 3 – Marriage of forces personnel under UK law

Part 3 provides for a power for Her Majesty by Order in Council to make provision for members of the armed forces serving overseas, and accompanying civilians, to marry in the presence of a chaplain or other authorised officer. Such an Order in Council would replace the

Foreign Marriage (Armed Forces) Order 1964, made under section 22 of the Foreign Marriage Act 1892, for both opposite sex and same sex couples. In respect of same sex couples the Order would authorise a marriage only where the couple would have been eligible to marry in a part of the United Kingdom to be determined in accordance with the Order. Thus the marriage of a same sex couple would be authorised only if the relevant part of the United Kingdom were one which permits such marriages. In relation to the marriage of a same sex couple the Order could also include provision prohibiting the use of particular religious rites or usages and will specifically preclude marriage according to the rites of the Church of England or the Church in Wales. The Order must also make provision as to consents to the solemnization of marriages of same sex couples according to other religious rites.

Part 4 – General provisions

Part 4 contains procedural provisions for making Orders in Council under this Schedule. Such Orders will be subject to the affirmative resolution procedure and may amend United Kingdom legislation. These provisions are necessary to provide a mechanism to amend existing legislation, in order that the procedures for consular marriage, provision of certificates of no impediment and armed forces overseas marriages can be modernised. Should the Orders in Council make provision which would otherwise be within the legislative competence of the Scottish Parliament, then Scottish Ministers must be consulted before the Order in Council is made.

Schedule 7 – Transitional and consequential provision etc

Part 1 – Transitional and transitory provision

Paragraph 1 deals with transitional arrangements in relation to "approved premises". These are premises (such as hotels) which have been approved by local authorities as venues for civil marriage ceremonies and civil partnership registrations. The effect of paragraph 1 is that any premises in the process of applying to be approved, or already approved, as a venue for marriages of opposite sex couples will automatically be approved as a venue for marriages of same sex couples. Any future applications for, and grants of, approval of premises, will be for both same sex and opposite sex civil marriage ceremonies. All approved premises will be subject to the approved premises regulations (as defined) and any related guidance, on commencement of section 11.

Part 2 – Minor and consequential amendments

Part 2 (paragraphs 2-21) makes amendments to the Marriage Act.

Paragraph 3 amends section 3 (Marriages of persons under 18) of the Marriage Act. The effect of this amendment is that a person who has previously been a civil partner and whose partner has died will not need to get parental consent for marrying another person even if he or she is under 18.

Paragraph 4 amends section 25 (Void marriages) to provide that marriages of same sex couples according to the rites of the Church of England will be void. Paragraph 5 amends section 27A of the Marriage Act to extend the provisions for requiring additional information for detained or house-bound marriages to such marriages of same sex couples.

Paragraph 6 inserts a new section 27D into the Marriage Act to provide that the superintendent registrar may require a copy of the relevant governing authority's consent in the cases of marriage of same sex couples in respect of Quaker marriages and marriages under the rites of the Jewish religion, and marriage of a house-bound or detained person.

Paragraph 7 amends section 28A of the Marriage Act to insert a power for the superintendent registrar to require the relevant governing authority to give evidence of the consent required for Quaker, Jewish or detained or house-bound marriages of same sex couples.

Paragraph 8 amends the title of section 41 of the Marriage Act to refer to a marriage of a man and a woman and applies the provisions of section 41 only to the marriage of a man and a woman.

Paragraph 9 amends section 42 of the Marriage Act dealing with cancellation of registration of premises no longer used, to apply this provision only to buildings registered to carry out marriages of opposite sex couples.

Paragraph 10 amends section 43 of the Marriage Act to take account of different statutory provisions which apply to the registration of religious buildings for marriages of same sex and opposite sex couples. The power to appoint an authorised person may be exercised within one year of the building's registration to solemnize marriages (whether marriages of an opposite sex or same sex couple).

Paragraphs 11 and 12 insert and amend internal cross-references in sections 44 and 45A of the Marriage Act regarding solemnization of marriages in registered buildings and solemnization of marriages at one of the parties' place of residence.

Paragraph 13 inserts new subsections (1A) to (1D) into section 46 of the Marriage Act to provide for a religious ceremony after a registrar's marriage of a same sex couple (except for the Church of England and Church in Wales) and providing the religious organisation has consented to such ceremonies.

Paragraph 14 makes consequential amendments to section 48 of the Marriage Act to ensure that a lack of consent to marriage of same sex couples or to registration of the building in which the marriage took place on the part of the relevant governing body does not affect the validity of the marriage.

Paragraph 15 inserts new section 49A which provides that a marriage of a same sex couple will be void if they have knowingly and wilfully married in the absence of the required consent to the marriage of same sex couples.

Paragraph 16 amends section 53 of the Marriage Act to provide that where a couple marry under the rites of the Jewish religion, the secretary of their synagogue registers the marriage and, where the couple are members of different synagogues, they can nominate which secretary registers their marriage.

Paragraph 17 inserts a reference to people authorised to register marriages of opposite sex couples into section 69 of the Marriage Act (Licensing of chapels for marriages according to the Church of England or Church in Wales).

Paragraph 18 inserts a reference to buildings registered to solemnize marriages of opposite sex couples into section 70 of the Marriage Act (which deals with the registration of chapels for marriages otherwise than according to the rites of the Church of England or the Church in Wales).

Paragraph 19 inserts references to marriage of same sex couples into section 75 of the Marriage Act (Offences relating to solemnization of marriage).

Paragraph 20 amends section 78 of the Marriage Act (Interpretation) to provide an amended definition of an "authorised person" to make clear how it applies in relation to both an opposite sex marriage ceremony and a same sex marriage ceremony and an updated definition of a "registered building". It also defines England and Wales legislation in the context of the Marriage Act.

Paragraph 21 amends Schedule 4 to the Marriage Act (Provisions of the Act excluded or modified in their application to Naval, Military and Air Force chapels) to insert references to provisions for marriage of same sex couples and provides a definition of England and Wales legislation for the Marriage Act.

Paragraphs 22 to 25 amend sections 1 and 2 of the Marriage (Registrar General's Licence) Act 1970 with the effect that the superintendent registrar has the power to require the governing authority of a religious body which proposes to conduct a "deathbed marriage" of a same sex couple to provide evidence of its consent to marriage of same sex couples. This ensures that equivalent religious protections are applied to these marriages, and gives the superintendent registrar the same powers to require evidence of consent in respect of deathbed marriages as he or she has for other marriages of same sex couples according to religious rites which do not take place on appropriately registered premises.

Paragraph 25 inserts a new section 13A which provides that, as for other marriages of same sex couples, a marriage of a same sex couple under the deathbed marriage provisions will be void, if they have knowingly and wilfully married in the absence of the required consent to the marriage of same sex couples.

Paragraphs 26 and 27 repeal section 11(c) of the Matrimonial Causes Act 1973 with the effect that the fact that a couple are not a man and a woman does not make a marriage void.

Paragraph 28 amends section 29JA of the Public Order Act 1986 to ensure that discussion or criticism of marriage which concerns the sex of the parties to it are not taken in themselves to be threatening or intended to stir up hatred.
Paragraphs 29 and 30 make consequential amendments to the Social Security Contributions and Benefits Act 1992.

Paragraphs 31 and 32 make consequential amendments to section 99 of the Pension Schemes Act 1993. Section 99 sets out the duties of trustees or managers of schemes after a member has exercised the option conferred by section 95 (Ways of taking right to cash equivalent). Section 99(3)(b) refers only to the pension or benefits of a member or his widow. Paragraph 32 amends section 99(3)(b) so that it applies to the pension and benefits of a member and his or her spouse or civil partner.

Paragraphs 33 to 36 amend the Civil Partnership Act.

Paragraph 34 amends the provisions in section 1(3) of the Civil Partnership Act, which set out how a civil partnership can be ended. The amendment provides that, in addition to death, dissolution and annulment, a civil partnership ends if it is converted into a marriage under section 9 of the Act.

Paragraph 35 amends section 4 of the Civil Partnership Act, which provides that, where a person wishing to register a civil partnership is under 18 years of age, the consent of an appropriate person or persons is required. Subsection 4(3) of the Civil Partnership Act currently provides that this requirement does not apply if the child is a surviving civil partner. The effect of this amendment is that a widow or widower under the age of 18 will not require the consent of another person before entering into a civil partnership.

Paragraph 45 amends paragraph 2 of Schedule 9 to the Equality Act 2010 (Religious requirements relating to sex, marriage etc, sexual orientation) so that, where employment is for the purposes of an organised religion, an occupational requirement may allow a restriction that a person should not be married to someone of the same sex. This means, for example, that a church may require that a priest not be married to a person of the same sex.

Commencement

219. The short title of the Act and the power to make commencement orders came into force on 17 July 2013 - the day on which the Act was passed (section 21), as did sections 15 and 16. The remaining

provisions of the Act will be brought into force on a day or days appointed by commencement order made by the Secretary of State and provisions may be brought into force on different days and at different times for different purposes.

****

Further information

Or the Women and Equality unit website at www.equalities.gov.uk

Stonewall can provide information on www.stonewall.org.uk

Northern Ireland information on civil partnerships and same sex marriages go to www.nidirect.uk

For information on civil partnerships and same sex marriages in Scotland go to www.civilpartnershipscotland.co.uk

Tax-contact your local tax office or go to www.hmrc.gov.uk

Pensions-contact the pension service on 0845 601293

Social security benefits-contact the benefit enquiry line on 0800 220674

Tax credits contact the tax Credits help line on 0913 232 1110

Child Benefit- contact the child Benefit Help line on 0300 200 3100

Child Support agency- contact 0845 713 3133

Adoption-for more information go to www.everchildmatters.gov.uk/socialcare/lookedafterchildren/adoption or contact your local council or voluntary adoption agency.

Immigration-contact the immigration and Nationality Directorate to www.ind.homeoffice.gov.uk

Relationship support – contact relate on 0300 100 1234

Domestic Violence – 0808 2000 247 24 hour Freephone www.nationaldomesticviolencehelpline.org.uk

Broken Rainbow-LGTB domestic violence forum on 0300 999 5428.

INDEX

171

Emerald Publishing
www.emeraldpublishing.co.uk

Titles in the Emerald Series:

Law

Guide to Bankruptcy
Conducting Your Own Court case
Guide to Consumer law
Creating a Will
Guide to Family Law
Guide to Employment Law
Guide to European Union Law
Guide to Health and Safety Law
Guide to Criminal Law
Guide to Landlord and Tenant Law
Guide to the English Legal System
Guide to Housing Law
Guide to Marriage and Divorce
Guide to The Civil Partnerships Act
Guide to The Law of Contract
The Path to Justice
You and Your Legal Rights
Powers of Attorney
Managing Divorce

Health

Guide to Combating Child Obesity
Asthma Begins at Home
Alternative Health and Alternative Remedies

Music

How to Survive and Succeed in the Music Industry

General

A Practical Guide to Obtaining probate
A Practical Guide to Residential Conveyancing
Writing The Perfect CV
Keeping Books and Accounts-A Small Business Guide
Business Start Up-A Guide for New Business
Finding Asperger Syndrome in the Family-A Book of Answers
Explaining Autism Spectrum Disorder
Explaining Alzheimers
Explaining Parkinsons
Writing True Crime
Becoming a Professional Writer
Writing your Autobiography

For details of the above titles published by Emerald go to:

www.emeraldpublishing.co.uk